SpringerBriefs in Computer Science

SpringerBriefs present concise summaries of cutting-edge research and practical applications across a wide spectrum of fields. Featuring compact volumes of 50 to 125 pages, the series covers a range of content from professional to academic.

Typical topics might include:

- A timely report of state-of-the art analytical techniques
- A bridge between new research results, as published in journal articles, and a contextual literature review
- A snapshot of a hot or emerging topic
- An in-depth case study or clinical example
- A presentation of core concepts that students must understand in order to make independent contributions

Briefs allow authors to present their ideas and readers to absorb them with minimal time investment. Briefs will be published as part of Springer's eBook collection, with millions of users worldwide. In addition, Briefs will be available for individual print and electronic purchase. Briefs are characterized by fast, global electronic dissemination, standard publishing contracts, easy-to-use manuscript preparation and formatting guidelines, and expedited production schedules. We aim for publication 8–12 weeks after acceptance. Both solicited and unsolicited manuscripts are considered for publication in this series.

**Indexing: This series is indexed in Scopus, Ei-Compendex, and zbMATH **

Jianfeng Xu • Shuliang Wang • Zhenyu Liu •
Yashi Wang • Yingfei Wang • Yingxu Dang

Objective Information Theory

 Springer

Jianfeng Xu
Information Technology Service
Center of People's Court
Beijing, China

Shuliang Wang
School of Computer Science and Technology
Beijing Institute of Technology
Beijing, China

Zhenyu Liu
School of Information Management
for Law
China University of Political Science
and Law
Beijing, China

Yashi Wang
School of Information Management
for Law
China University of Political Science
and Law
Beijing, China

Yingfei Wang
Information Technology Service
Center of People's Court
Beijing, China

Yingxu Dang
School of Computer Science and Technology
Beijing Institute of Technology
Beijing, China

This work was supported by Information Technology Service Center of People's Court

ISSN 2191-5768   ISSN 2191-5776   (electronic)
SpringerBriefs in Computer Science
ISBN 978-981-19-9928-4   ISBN 978-981-19-9929-1   (eBook)
https://doi.org/10.1007/978-981-19-9929-1

This Springer imprint is published by the registered company Springer Nature Singapore Pte Ltd.
The registered company address is: 152 Beach Road, #21-01/04 Gateway East, Singapore 189721, Singapore

Foreword

Information is an indispensable component of our daily life and plays an ever more central role as we enter the information age. The rapid development of information technologies such as cloud computing, Internet of Things, mobile Internet, big data, and artificial intelligence has increased the scale and complexity of information systems. The numerous information systems in the real world have or will profoundly change our way of working and daily life. The widespread applications of information technology and systems have led to broadly significant progress in the Information Society.

However, our understanding of information itself is still very limited. Although great progress has been made in information theory since the pioneering work of Shannon in 1948, there is still no consensus on information in the wide sense concerning its model and measurement, let alone the nature of the information. Shannon's theory is hugely successful in the application to communication systems, but also limited to that. As Shannon himself put it as the title of his original paper "A mathematical theory of communication," his theory was developed mainly for the purpose of communication engineering, and it would be wishful thinking to expect that this theory also works for other systems involving information.

In his celebrated book *Cybernetics or Control and Communication in the Animal and the Machine* published in 1948, Wiener pointed out the pivotal importance of feedback information in the control of both biological and man-made systems. Decades of studies in control theory have found that the relation between feedback information and system controllability is much more complicated than explicable by Shannon's framework. Significant advances in biological sciences also uncovered many more complicated roles information plays in natural systems. For example, the information buried in the DNA sequence is far richer than the number of bits can describe.

Information systems abound in practice. The authors of this book have many years of experience in developing and researching information systems. In particular, Prof. Xu Jianfeng has been leading the nationwide construction, application, and promotion of the Smart Court system-of-systems engineering project of China, which guarantees the continuous upgrading of the level of informatization and reshaping of the judicial operation pattern of Chinese courts. These experiences have led the authors to a more profound view of the nature of information, and in particular, how information is measured in information systems.

In this book, Prof. Xu and his coauthors propose the concept of objective information, which is depicted from a philosophical view, a formal assumption, and a corresponding mathematical model. Furthermore, to demonstrate the feasibility of applying the objective information theory in the practice of large-scale complex information system constructions, two exemplificative cases of the air traffic control system and the Smart Court project of China are demonstrated. Therefore, this book provides a reference approach to quantitatively analyzing information operations in complex information system applications. Also, this book can serve as a textbook for senior students and graduate students in related majors.

I hope that Prof. Xu and his research team will continue to deepen the study of objective information theory and continue to make new progress in the development of information science.

Chinese Academy of Sciences,   Lei Guo
Beijing, China

Preface

Information is inseparable from an information society. The rapid development of information technologies such as cloud computing, Internet of Things, mobile Internet, big data, and artificial intelligence has increased the scale of information systems. The numerous information systems in the objective world have or will profoundly change human production and lifestyles. The popular applications of information technology and system bring a broad significance in the progress towards the information society.

People have made contributions to understanding and using information such as information theory. The information theory on change describes how things vary. It emphasizes the difference in size, amount, degree, or nature for telling an exact object from common objects. For example, Shannon defined information with the mathematical equation and made continuous contributions. He revealed the fundamentals of information transmission with probability and statistical methods for communication systems. However, there is no consensus on understanding information. It is difficult to distinguish the relationship between objectively existing information and subjective conscious activities. The measurement on information is inconsistent, leading to the problem of "difficult to model, difficult to measure, and difficult to evaluate" in the design, development, and application of complex information systems with big data. It has become a bottleneck to restrict the vigorous development and implementation of information systems in the national informatization strategy.

Actually, information is the link that connects everything in the world. Everything can express existence and movement through its objective reflection in the world. Information may reflect the existence, characteristics, and movement states of matter, and further helps matter interact with each other. In the implementation of information system engineering, information integration mirrors the static characteristics and dynamic changes of things. What information systems deal with is all kinds of objective information reflected in it, and does not first define whether it changes or not. The acquisition, transmission, processing, storage, and application of information may have not only individual function but also collective impact on the large-scale information systems. To understand the information from the view of reflection instead of change, we proposed objective information theory.

In this book, the objective information is depicted from the philosophical view, formal assumption, and mathematical model. Information is defined to reflect the world with the properties of objectivity, restorability, transitivity, combination, and relevance in the context of the sextuple model and mapping theory. By analyzing the similarities and dissimilarities between objective information and subjective knowledge, it uses mathematical language to give a sextuple model of information, discusses the basic properties of information, makes the definition of information more rigorous and clearer, and analyzes information systems. The metric system of objective information is presented in mainly 11 indicators: volume, delay, scope, granularity, variety, duration, sampling rate, aggregation, coverage, distortion, and mismatch. Each metric indicator is mathematically defined from the basic model with specific properties. To demonstrate the feasibility and practicality to investigate complex information systems at large scale with big data, the exemplification of the objective information theory takes Air Traffic Control System (ATCS) and Smart Court. The results show that objective information theory provides an alternative tool to fully master and take advantage of quantitative analysis of information operation in complex and uncertain scenarios, and precise control of information system applications. Especially, Xu Jianfeng put the objective information theory into the nationwide construction, application and promotion of the Smart Court system-of-systems engineering project of China for guaranteeing the upgrade and reshaping of the judicial operation pattern of Chinese courts. It has gained remarkable achievements and brought China to the leading position in judicial informatization in the world.

The work in this book is funded by the National Key R&D Program of China (2016YFC0800801, 2020YFC0832600) and National Natural Science Fund of China (62076027).

Many scholars have provided a lot of help for the writing of this book. Here, I would like to express our heartfelt thanks.

Beijing, China   Jianfeng Xu
November 2022   Shuliang Wang
                                                                              Zhenyu Liu
                                                                              Yashi Wang
                                                                            Yingfei Wang
                                                                            Yingxu Dang

Contents

Chapter 1
Information Theory on Change
to Reflection

Abstract Information reflects the existence, basic characteristics, and movement states of matter in the world. In the information society, it is difficult for human activities to leave information for the wide application of information technologies and systems bring a broad significance. Having achievements in both theory and application, information theory can be divided into the information theory on change and the information theory on reflection on the basis of cognitive perspective. In this chapter, the objective information theory (OIT) will be introduced to the background and motivation. It starts from the information theory on change. The bottleneck problems are discussed on information science, and information system. Then, the information theory on reflection is put forward. Two theories are further discriminated from the perspective of information. Finally, the monograph contents are briefed.

Keywords The information theory on change · The information theory on reflection · The state of the art

1.1 The Information Theory on Change

In the development of information theory, Harry Nyquist and Ralph Vinton Lyon Hartley have seminal role in the information theory, in the light of which Shannon defines information with the mathematical equation and made continuous contributions. They lay foundation for quantitative calculation and rapid development of the information theory on change.

1.1.1 Information Communication

In an early stage, the information describes how the things vary because of the initial knowledge and low calculations. To mathematically clarify the nature of communication, Harry Nyquist made fundamental theoretical and practical contributions to telecommunications. He [1] analyzed the relationship between the speed of a

J. Xu et al., *Objective Information Theory*, SpringerBriefs in Computer Science,
https://doi.org/10.1007/978-981-19-9929-1_1

telegraph system and the number of signal values used by the communication system. His principles of sampling continuous signals to convert them to digital signals [2], showed that the sampling rate must be at least twice the highest frequency present in the sample in order to reconstruct the original signal.

To establish a quantitative measure to compare the capacities of various communication-systems to transmit information, Ralph Vinton Lyon Hartley [3] distinguished between meaning and information. Information was defined as the number of possible messages, independent of whether they are meaningful. He further thought that messages are concrete and diverse symbols, and information is the abstract parameter in the messages. Under the umbrella of this definition of information, he gave a logarithmic law for the transmission of information in discrete messages. With the logarithm of the probability on a message occurrence to measure information, he took sample from a set of symbols to create a word. If the probability of each symbol is the same, and the selection is random, you can get different words. In 1955, he further presented the information theory of the Fourier analysis and wave mechanics.

Claude Elwood Shannon [4] acknowledged his debt to works by Nyquist and Hartley in the first paragraph of his paper *"The Mathematical Theory of Communication"*. He believed that the basic problem of communication was to accurately or approximately reproduce the message selected by another point at one point. Information is defined as a set of codes that encode the probability of occurrence of events, and the uncertainty of information is measured by using an entropy. A model of the communication system was given to solve the technical problems on accurately transmitting communication symbols, such as information capacity, statistical features of information sources, information source coding, channel coding, information measurement, and the relationship between channel capacity and noise.

As a result, for the first time in history, mankind clearly understood and grasped the essence of communication technology, which promoted the vigorous development of communication systems. Therefore, the information theory pays attention to the message transmission in information communication. The change of the symbol values transmits the message. The logarithm of the probability on a message occurrence models the information measurement.

1.1.2 Typical achievements of the information theory on change

Nowadays, there are many contributions to the information theory on change. The representative is Shannon information theory [4], including full information theory [5], general information theory [6, 7], representation information theory [8], unified information theory [9, 10], and information geometry theory [11]. These achievements strongly promoted human society from the industrial age to the information age.

Shannon Information Theory

The idea is to extract the information from countless events. Information was described as "a group of codes with the probability of occurrence $p_1, p_2, \ldots, p_n$" with the entropy [4].

$$H(X) = H(p_1, p_2, \cdots, p_n) = -k \sum_{i=1}^{n} p_i \log p_i \tag{1.1}$$

It is a measure that reflects the uncertainty of information and lays the theoretical foundation of Shannon information theory. Sequentially, Wiener [12], Ashby [13], De Luca, and Termini [14] used their entropy equations to measure information. Shannon entropy was further expanded, i.e. cumulative residual entropy [15–17], joint entropy [18, 19], conditional entropy [20–22], exponential entropy [23], mutual information entropy [24, 25], cross entropy [26–28], maximum entropy principle [29, 30] and so on. These results have prompted the development of information entropy.

Expansion from Shannon Information Theory

Zhong Yixin [5] proposed full information theory by taking "self-representation/ self-revealing of the state of things and state changes" as the definition of information at the ontological level. He believes that full information includes the epistemological level information of the external form, internal meaning and utility value of the movement state of things and their changing modes. To truly master the epistemological information of the matter, you have to perceive its form, understand its meaning, and know its value. Simultaneously considering three factors, the formal is grammatical information, the meaning is semantic information, and the utility is pragmatic information.

General information theory [6, 7] treated information as the ability to cause changes under the principles of noumenon and value. In a information logic system IF(R), a mathematical model of triples was $\langle C, I, R \rangle$, where C is information carrier, I is information, and R is the system that information belongs to. A series of operators between C, I, R and IF(R) are used to transmit, receive, and store information. Taking information, carrier, and belonging system as a complete system, general information theory opens a door to study the nature and operation of information by using mathematical methods. Moreover, three types of structural metrics are given to measure the degree of information change: internal, intermediate, and external. They are namely abstract, reality, and experiment, defined under different target and requirement.

Representation information theory [8] is the proportion of structural complexity changes caused by a group of objects removed from their categories, by understandings the principles of human concept communication and learning. Compared with

Shannon information theory, there are some expansions. The first is to replace the symbol sequence with the conceptual structure. The second is to replace the probability with the category invariance. And the third is replaces simple events with a collection of group objects.

Unified information theory [9, 10] uses a consistent concept to contain many different information connotations. It describes information as the structure, state, or state of the system, considering information from grammatical to semantic and pragmatic state. Its analysis of the product of behavior change is like full information theory [5], while the theoretical depth and systematisms are far inferior to the latter.

Information Geometry

In contrast with Shannon information entropy, information geometry theory is known as the second generation of information theory [31]. It contaminates probability statistics and geometric methods. Rao [32] used the geodesic distance to measure the difference between the probability distribution functions by defining the Riemann metric on the manifold with Fisher information matrix [33]. Efron [34] gave the curvature on the statistical manifold. Chentsov [35] presented a family of affine connections on the statistical manifold. Amari [36] proposed the concept of dual affine connections.

1.1.3   The Limitations of the Information Theory on Change

The information theory on change emphasizes the difference in size, amount, degree, or nature for telling an exact object from common objects. However, many researchers lack an outline and consistent consensus on the objects, purposes, and methods of information. People's understanding of information is still divided, and the measurement on information is also inconsistent.

Regarding the object to study information, it is difficult to distinguish the relationship between objectively existing information and people's subjective conscious activities. The information in people's minds belongs to both objective and subjective categories, which is extremely complicated.

With regard to the purpose to study information, academic exploration and deduction are satisfied with. To a large extent, they ignore the numerous information systems in the objective world that have or will profoundly change human production and lifestyles. They also neglect the impact of acquisition, transmission, processing, storage and application in a information system, especially the actual guiding role of the research, design and development of large-scale integrated information systems.

For the method to study information, Shannon traditional probability and statistics methods for communication systems are inherited, which limits the proposal of more feasible and extensive method to comprehensively and systematically establish the theoretical foundation of information science. Furthermore, in the information theory represented by Shannon, the basic view is that only when the recipient of the information receives the information, the information can produce meaning.

1.2   Bottleneck Problems in Information Science

In an information system, information is integrated to reflect the static characteristics and dynamic changes of matter, which is a whole and difficult to separate in the real world. Nowadays, it is a trend to integrate, or make use of, different information systems to build a larger-scale system. However, there are various concepts on information with different connotations in information science. Lacking an outline on the objects, purposes, and methods, no consensus on the theory of information comes into being. The metrics is not systematic. It is difficult to guide the giant project.

1.2.1   Different Concept Descriptions

The pronouns of early information are with a certain meaning. The production, transmission and utilization of information is a human instinct. After the 1920s, with the large-scale production in the industrial age and the development of science and technology, the amount of information has increased rapidly. With the rapid increase in the amount of social information, people have to study how to obtain, process, transmit and use information in a timely and accurate manner. Some people go to explore information, and various definitions have been put forward for information.

- Information is a state that can be described in the form of numerical values, words, sounds, images, etc.;
- Information is an objective phenomenon described and represented by data as a carrier.
- Information is the result of data processing and extraction, and is also useful knowledge for humans.
- Information is a message with a certain meaning implicit in a physical signal;
- The purpose of signal processing is to obtain useful information from the signal.

In general terms, information is an objective phenomenon that can be described, and it is also knowledge with a certain physical meaning.

As Shannon said, "The basic results of information theory (in the narrow sense) are all aimed at some very special problems. They may not be suitable for psychology, economics, and some other social science fields." The limitations of the special information theory are mainly manifested in the three aspects:

- Firstly, the form of information is considered, neglecting the meaning and value of information. This problem cannot be avoided when processing and using information;
- Secondly, it is limited to the category of eliminating random uncertainty under probability theory by studying a random process with clear boundaries between right and wrong. Actually, it is more of the fuzzy phenomenon of "this and the other". These universal ambiguities cannot be solved with the information theory in the narrow sense;
- Thirdly, statistical information is considered more than non-statistical information. The information transmission is involved, ignoring other information processes that are broader and more important.

1.2.2 Different Essential Connotation

There is a significant difference between objective information and subjective cognition. People can recognize, describe, and use information, but they cannot change information with their own subjective thoughts. Even if people have different interpretations of information under their respective subject areas and knowledge background, the objectivity of the source and content of information cannot be denied. As the material is not transferred by human will, the objectivity of information is also not shift with people's thoughts. Facing the same objective information, there various subjective cognition.

- Objective information exists on the objects, while subjective cognition is in the brain. Objective information is in the form of written or spoken language on paper, sound waves in the air, electromagnetic signals in the tape recorder, and so on. But subjective cognition only exists in human brain.
- Objective information is easy to perceive, while subjective cognition is difficult to perceive. People can smoothly perceive the specific content of objective information through light and sound. But the cognitive process of participants can be reflected to a certain extent through the content of their retelling, and it is difficult to be strictly and accurately determined from the difference of information before and after measurement.
- The state of objective information is stable, while the one of subjective cognition is complicated. Objective information may be recorded on paper or audio, and its specific content could be maintained for a long period of time. However, the differences in various reported content showed obvious irregularities, which reflected subjective cognition on the complexity of change.
- Objective information is easy to repeat, while subjective cognition changes with time. It is easy to repetitively use the same objective information under various circumstances at different time. But the results of them may different from each other, reflecting the time-varying effect of subjective cognition due to changes in subjective information and objective conditions.

There are indeed fundamental differences between objective information and subjective cognition. People have to change the purpose, theories, methods and means of studying objective information and subjective cognition. Relatively, it is more intuitive, simpler and easier to study objective information than subjective cognition. So it is necessary to distinguish the objective and subjective attributes of information, and to define information in the category of objectivity.

1.2.3 Difficulty to Guide the Giant Project

It is difficult to adapt to the current needs of informatization when evaluating the effectiveness of complex systems such as operating status, fault discovery and handling. Good correspondence and quantification are the basis to build and evaluate a complex information system. A metric system with multiple indicators may lead to the improvement of overall construction effectiveness. The application effectiveness is the core to build a quality-efficiency indicator system, but there is still a lack of an indicator system to measure the quality and efficiency of complex system informatization. People have to pay attention to the operational quality and operational effectiveness of the complex system under the informatization. The traditional index system is often oriented to the quality of system equipment, such as resource allocation and failure occurrence. Nowadays, it imperative to develop the performance indicators for specific fields under the information metrics of information systems, so as to provide benchmark guidance for comprehensively analyzing, implementing and evaluating the complex system.

System-of-systems (SoS) is a system composed of a series of complex systems [37]. SoS engineering implementation combines many systems with independent operation, independent management, location distribution, emergent behavior and gradual development. The process not only maintains their respective independence, but also realizes more and stronger capabilities of the whole system. When various complex systems converge to form an SoS, it is necessary to further enrich and deepen related theories and methods to effectively solve main problems such as integration, sharing, coordination, evaluation and optimization.

To achieve a wider range and a higher level of sharing and collaboration, it is essential to optimize the overall performance of SoS under the basic requirements when integrating various systems. So it is necessary to effectively bridge the gap between the comprehensive integration of large-scale SoS and individual development of various systems. It may clearly expresses and maintains various information relationships among different systems without bogged down by tedious details, and reasonably balances the allocation of tasks. With the expansion of an SoS, it is important to reshape the original business model in an all-round way that the capacity and effectiveness of SoS as a whole can be improved from local to global, from short-term to lasting, and from relatively simple ideal settings to complex practical environments, through continuous quality-effectiveness analysis with key performance indicators and popularization, in order to achieve a good state of stability, universality, long-term operation, continuous evolution and continuous improvement.

According to the top-level design of the complex system, the system-level components of the complex system can be obtained, and each system-level component is an information system that manages objective information. The rapid development of information technologies such as cloud computing, Internet of Things, mobile Internet, big data, and artificial intelligence has increased the scale of information systems. Furthermore, the super-large-scale complex system needs to consider more factors, such as high-dimensional, multi-source, heterogeneous, nonlinear, uncertain, etc., making the information system more and more complex, and fewer and fewer problems can be solved correctly. Many problems need to be solved approximately by numerical calculation methods. The information system has encountered a major theoretical bottleneck of "difficult to model, difficult to measure, and difficult to calculate".

The operation of a complex system is a typical complex giant system problem. The factors that affect the results of the operation include basic equipment factors, user behavior factors, etc., and there are many cross-influences between each other. When the information system transitions from big data to strong intelligence, the scale of the information system becomes larger and more complex. As the scale and complexity of informatization in various industries continue to expand, such as air traffic control systems, Smart Court, etc. Focusing on the equipment of the complex system and taking fault handling as the goal, it has been difficult to adapt to the current needs of informatization. How to ensure the high-quality, efficient operation, and great value of informatization has become the focus of attention in the complex system.

The information theory on change said that it is impossible to effectively evaluate and guide the efficiency and capabilities of complex information systems and intelligent computing, which severely restricts the depth and breadth of the construction and application of big data intelligent information systems, and it has been difficult to fully satisfy big data. The increasingly complex and huge needs of intelligent systems have made it difficult to support the sustainable development of the complex world. It is urgent to break through the original shackles of information theory.

1.3   The Information Theory on Reflection

Information is the constituent element of the world, and it also reflects the nature of things in the world and the laws of their movement. In a information space, the real world is the essence and true nature of the information space, and provides the source of all information. In turn, the information space reflects the real world and feedbacks the real world by simulating and deducing objects and movements that are costly to conduct physically.

1.3.1 The Objective World and the Subjective World

The world is divided into two categories: the subjective world and the objective world [38]. Generally, the subjective world refers to the world of consciousness and ideas, and is the sum of the spiritual and psychological activities of understanding and grasping the entire world. It includes both the process of consciousness activities and the results of consciousness activities. Human concepts, will, desires, emotions, beliefs, etc., are different forms and manifestations of the subjective world. It relies on mankind's active thinking and awareness of the objective world, mainly cognition, understanding, control and utilization, and is the unity of knowledge, affection, and intention. The objective world refers to the material and perceivable world, which is the sum of all matter and its movement outside of conscious activities. It can be divided into two parts: natural existence and social existence. The former does not depend on anything but exists objectively, and the latter is formed in the process of human social practice but is not transferred by human will. The objective world does not depend on people's subjective consciousness. It is mainly the connotative nature of the world and the law of extensional motion, rather than a collection of consciousness and concepts.

The objective world and the subjective world are related and distinguished. The information in the objective world can act on the subjective world. We can treat the consciousness, concepts, thinking, and decision-making formed by humans and even other students from the information of the objective world as information. Owing to the objectivity of information, people can collect, transmit, process, aggregate, and apply information with various means. The rapid development of emerging technologies, such as artificial intelligence, brain-like systems, and brain–computer interfaces, is driven by advances that simulate the human mind and then transform humanity's subjective processes into objective information that can be processed by information systems. At the same time, there are still many essential differences between information in the objective world and consciousness or concepts in the subjective world.

The subjective world consciousness and the objective world information are heterogeneous. The objective world exists outside of human conscious activities, has direct reality, and moves according to its own inherent laws. The information it reflects is objectively existing, but it is different for different subjects. The material basis of external natural existence lies, and the material basis of human social existence is the material production method. Consciousness exists in the human brain, which is extensive and stretchable, and is mainly reflected in the spirit and thinking activities. In this sense, the subjective world is the range and boundary of the intelligence, wisdom, and thinking ability of the subject's conscious activities, as well as the range of thinking capacity that it can accept, understand, and process information. This also directly leads to individual differences, and different subjects may have different understandings when dealing with the same objective information.

On the other hand, the subjective world and the objective world are opposed and unified. Generally speaking, the objective world determines the subjective world, and the objective world is the external space of the subjective world. However, the subjective world is a kind of conscious existence after all. People can assemble and construct objects at will within consciousness, so that the subjective world can not only be the expression and reflection of the objective world, but also deviate from the objective world in some aspects, or even transcend the objective world. The world makes predictions for the future based on existing information. This has led to the incomplete synchronization of the development of the subjective world and the objective world. The subjective world and the objective world have a complicated contradictory relationship. On the one hand, the subjective world affirms and reflects the objective world; on the other hand, it deviates, denies, and transcends the objective world. The two are always intertwined.

Popper [39] further proposed three worlds. The first world is the world of physical objects or physical states composed of all matter and various phenomena in the objective world; the second world is the world of consciousness or mental state, or the world of behavioral intentions about activities; and the third world is the world of the objective content of thoughts. Actually, the third world is the world of human spiritual products, especially the world of scientific thoughts, poetic thoughts, and works of art, and especially emphasized the objective reality and independence of the third world.

Knowledge is the previously unknown patterns in the objective sense or in the subjective recognition. When people produce objective knowledge through subjective spirit, the third world becomes an objective reality, and its existence separates from human beings and exists alone. It can be seen that Popper's first world and third world are actually a further division of the objective world, that is, the first world contains a part of objective information, the second world is the subjective world in the usual sense, and the third world is completely composed of objective information. Composition, regardless of whether people are aware of the content of these thoughts, they all exist autonomously.

1.3.2 Trinity of the Objective World

In the objective world that does not depend on human subjective consciousness, matter, energy, information are its three major constituent elements, which is also called the ternary nature of the objective world. Wiener [12] pointed out that "information is information, not matter or energy." Steucke [40] deepened this view and said that "information is the third thing alongside matter and energy". Thus formed the world's material, energy, and information "trilogy". In fact, the world here refers to the objective world, and does not include the subjective world, because matter and energy obviously only belong to the category of the objective world.

Information is the third thing juxtaposed with matter and energy. It reflects the existence and movement of matter. The world is material, matter is in motion, and motion is regular. The true unity of the world lies in its materiality. From the perspective of nature, things are formed and developed under their own inherent laws, have their own origin and development history, and are all components of a unified material world. Human society is also the long-term development of the material world. Heraclitus said that "one cannot step into the same river twice." The whole world is the eternally moving material world. The movement in philosophy refers to the changes and processes of all things, which are the inherent attributes of matter and the form of matter existence. Everything is in motion. Some movement is obvious, and people can directly feel it, such as moving cars, flowing rivers, piercing meteors, etc. Some change slowly, and it is not easy to notice, for example, Mount Everest has risen 1600 m in 500,000 years. The laws of nature are mostly expressed as dynamic laws, revealing the one-to-one correspondence between certain things, and pointing out that the existence of one kind of thing must lead to the occurrence of another certain thing. The law of social development is mainly manifested as the law of statistics, which reveals not a simple one-to-one correspondence between things, but a regular relationship between a certain inevitability and a variety of random phenomena [41].

In the ternary nature of the objective world, matter is an objective existence that does not depend on human subjective consciousness but can be reflected by human consciousness. From the new perspective of the trinity of matter, energy, and information in the real world, energy is the material movement ability that does not depend on human subjective consciousness, and information uses matter or energy as a medium. Information reflects the material nature, internal connections and movement patterns of natural and human things in the objective and subjective worlds. In short, matter is the existence of origin, energy is the existence of movement ability, and information is the existence of the connection of things. All kinds of physical information systems can and can only acquire, transmit, process and apply various objectively existing information. Dynamics are essentially the mathematical expression of the regularities and mechanics of motion and change in space and time [42–45]. It is crucial to comprehensively study the principles of information movement and utilization from the overall perspective of the real world, society, and information systems. Therefore, the cognition of ternary nature satisfies the objective requirements of the operating objects of the information system. These views are completely based on the objective reality of information, which helps the birth of objective information theory [42].

1.3.3 Contributions from Objective Information Theory

Objective information theory (OIT) gives a philosophical view that information is the objective reflection of things and their motion states in the objective and subjective world. It presents the concept of information, mathematical definition,

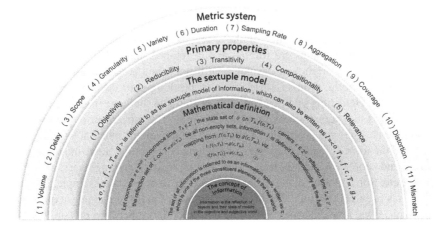

Fig. 1.1 Definition, model, nature and metric system of information [43]

sextuple model, primary properties, and metric systems (see Fig. 1.1) for conducting profound and quantitative investigations.

The first is to clearly define the essence of information in the objective category. In response to the diverse conceptual connotations and lack of a comprehensive metric system of information, OIT studies the methods of information reflecting the nature of things in the world and the laws of their movements. It not only conforms to the fundamental positioning of information as one of the three major components of the objective world, but also adapts to the operational requirements that information systems can and can only process objective and real information. Since the information in people's minds belongs to both objective and subjective categories, many studies do not distinguish the relationship between objective information and subjective conscious activities, which makes the problem extremely complicated. OIT focuses on simplifying the complex, decoupling the objective and subjective attributes of information to a certain extent, and combining the operational requirements of the information system.

The second is to put forward the mathematical expression of information and the sextuple model, which provide a unified, clear, convenient and feasible mathematical theory basis for all subsequent studies. Based on the objective reality of information, the definition of information is proposed. Information is an objective reflection of things and their movement in the objective world and subjective world. In the light of the definition, the sextuple model of information includes noumenon, state occurrence time, state function carrier, reflection time, and reflection function. This model deconstructs the concept of information in three important ways: the dual deconstruction of information subjects, the temporal deconstruction of information duration, and the form deconstruction of information contents. Through these three important deconstructions, we can not only measure the capacity of information, but also other aspects of the information more profoundly, comprehensively and quantitatively.

The third is the information sextuple model combines the internal characteristics and external needs of information. It embodies the rationality of information and its model definition. Through the proof of the basic nature of the information, the model is further improved. It defines information as the reflection from a state set to a reflection set. Objectivity is the constraint of information perception. restorability refers to the fundamental premise of information application. Transitivity is the basic mode of information transmission. Relevance is the important meaning of information existence. Combinability proves that information has a combinatorial nature.

The fourth is that an information metric system is inferred from the sextuple model and the basic properties of information. The metric system of objective information mainly includes 11 indicators: volume, delay, scope, granularity, variety, duration, sampling rate, aggregation, coverage, distortion, and mismatch. The entire system is more comprehensive, and there is independence between measurements. Each metric is expressed in quantitative forms such as the measurement, potential and distance of a specific element. Each element is in several metrics. It provides a basis for quantitative research and analysis of information operation and application of information systems. The significance of such metric system is that it provides important measurement guidance for the evaluation of information systems, apart from providing the ground for information measurement. As the main efficacies of information systems depend on the input and output information, the benchmark for judging information systems should be based on the evaluation indicators of these input and output information.

1.4   Discrimination of Two Information Views

Information is the blood, food, and vitality of the world [46]. The achievements of information have promoted human society from the industrial age to the information age [47]. But people's understanding of information is various, and measuring information is also inconsistent consensus [38]. There is a lack of the widely adopted mathematical expressions to describe the concept of information.

The information theory on change believes that information can only produce meaning when the recipient of the information receives the information. The representative is Shannon information theory. It reveals that the capacity of information in communication systems can be defined as entropy, which has led many people to mathematically regard information as negative entropy. Probability theory and stochastic processes are taken as basic research tools to study the entire process of the generalized communication system, rather than the entire link. At present, there are still research directions such as the deepening of information concepts, the development of information distortion theory and its application in data compression, and the basic theories of computer-centric information processing systems. However, the concept of information is far beyond that in communication systems. Information entropy, as an information expression, cannot meet the general requirements of information science and technology. Shannon information theory cannot effectively evaluate and guide the efficiency and capabilities of information systems and intelligent computing increasing complexity. Scholars are far from reaching a consensus on the nature of information, which is considered as the key obstruction in developing a unified, convenient, and feasible mathematical information foundation. This severely restricts the depth and breadth of the construction and application of intelligent information systems in the era of big data.

The information theory on reflection think that information reflects the nature of things and the laws of their movement, regardless of whether things change or not. The representative is objective information theory. It defines the sextuple model and 11 metric indicators of information to depict the elements and characteristics in the complex information system. Its mathematical foundations are set theory, measurement theory, and topology. Although these theories are relatively abstract, they have a direct and clear correspondence with the statistics and calculation methods widely used by people every day. It is fully applicable to various specific tasks that are generally required in the process of informatization, such as big data, information stream, and information system design and evaluation.

The appearance of the two views of information theory has specific background. Before Shannon information theory, digital communication has made certain developments. With the mathematical principles of communication to create information theory, Shannon brought mankind into the information age and promoted the rapid development of information technology. In the twenty first century, with the development of communication hardware, the birth of big data has brought huge innovations to information systems. Big data has massive volume, a wide variety of categories, a relatively low value density, and a rapid growth rate. The infrastructures for big data have put forward new technical requirements. Shannon information theory on change cannot provide an ideal theoretical description of the complex information system on big data products. To sum up the previous theoretical results and current information changes, Xu Jianfeng et al. proposes objective information theory to revolve around the operating quality and results of complex information systems in the era of big data. From the new perspective of the trinity of matter, energy and information in the real world, it studies the methods of information reflecting the nature of things in the world and the laws of movement. It tries to solve the fundamental theoretical issues such as the nature of information, measurement methods, model algorithms, and computational controllability for the precise control of the applicable evolution, the quantitative calculation, and the inference of information patterns in information systems. Its completeness and practicality will also be tested and revised in many subsequent applications, because any kind of theories can reflect their value and be perfected only in practice.

1.5 Chapter Summary

Everything in the world can express existence and movement through its objective reflection, that is, information. Information helps things interact with each other. So information can be viewed at the same value as matter and energy, and it is one-third of the world. People have understood the importance of information, and achieved fruitful results on research and applications. In particular, Shannon revealed the fundamentals of information transmission, and made outstanding contributions to human beings' progress towards an information society; Zhong Yixin proposed the theory of total information, opening a door for the in-depth interaction of information with human cognition and intelligence. Under the axiomatization, Burgin established the model and operator system of general information theory, providing a demonstration for the use of mathematical tools to study the nature and operation of information. Based on previous results, this chapter explores the information connotation from the information theory on change to the information theory on reflection. There is no consensus on the conceptual description, essential connotation, and theoretical level, especially if the measurement system is not a system, it is difficult to guide the implementation of information system engineering. In complex information systems, information integration reflects the static characteristics and dynamic changes of things, and it is necessary to solve fundamental theoretical problems in information science, such as information essence, measurement methods, model algorithms, and controllability of calculations.

References

1. Nyquist, H.: Certain factors affecting telegraph speed. J. Am. Inst. Elect. Eng. **43**(12), 1197–1198 (1924)
2. Nyquist, H.: Certain topics in telegraph transmission theory. Trans. Am. Inst. Electr. Eng. **47**(2), 617–644 (1928)
3. Hartley, R.V.L.: Transmission of information. Bell Syst. Tech. J. **7**, 535–563 (1928)
4. Shannon, C.E.: The mathematical theory of communication. Bell Syst. Tech. J. **27**(1), 379–423 (1948)
5. Zhong, Y.: Principles of Information Science. Beijing University of Posts and Telecommunications Press, Beijing (2002)
6. Burgin, M.: Information theory, a multifaceted model of information. Entropy. **5**(2), 146–160 (2003)
7. Burgin, M.: Theory of Information, Fundamentality, Diversity and Unification. World Scientific Publishing, Singapore (2010)
8. Vigo, R.: Representational information, a new general notion and measure of information. Inf. Sci. **181**(21), 4847–4859 (2011)
9. Fleissner, P., Hofkirchner, W.: Emergent information: towards a unified information theory. Biosystems. **38**(2), 243–248 (1996)
10. Capurro, R., Fleissner, P., Hofkirchner, W.: Is a unified theory of information feasible? A trialogue: in the request for unified theory of information. In: Proceeding of the Second International Conference on the Foundations of Information Science, pp. 9–30. Springer, Amsterdam (1999)

11. Rao, C.R.: Information and accuracy attainable in the estimation of statistical parameters. Bull. Calcutta Math. Soc. **37**, 81–91 (1945)
12. Wiener, N.: Cybernetics, or the Control and Communication in the Animal and the Machine. The MIT Press, Cambridge (1961)
13. Ashby, W.R.: An Introduction to Cybernetics. Chapman & Hall, London (1956)
14. De Luca, A., Termini, S.: A definition of nonprobabilistic entropy in the setting of fuzzy sets theory. Inf. Control. **20**(4), 301–312 (1972)
15. Rao, M., Chen, Y., Vemuri, B.C., et al.: Cumulative residual entropy: a new measure of information. IEEE Trans. Inf. Theory. **50**(6), 1220–1228 (2004)
16. Asadi, M., Zohrevand, Y.: On the dynamic cumulative residual entropy. J. Stat. Plan. Inf. **137**(6), 1931–1941 (2007)
17. Kumar, V., Taneja, H.C.: Some characterization results on generalized cumulative residual entropy measure. Stat. Prob. Lett. **81**(8), 1072–1077 (2011)
18. Abbas, A.E.: Entropy methods for joint distributions in decision analysis. IEEE Trans. Eng. Manag. **53**(1), 146–159 (2006)
19. Madiman, M., Tetali, P.: Information inequalities for joint distributions, with interpretations and applications. IEEE Trans. Inf. Theory. **56**(6), 2699–2713 (2010)
20. Gupta, G., Chaturvedi, A.: Conditional entropy based user selection for multiuser MIMO systems. IEEE Commun. Lett. **17**(8), 1628–1631 (2013)
21. Ho, S.W., Verdú, S.: On the interplay between conditional entropy and error probability. IEEE Trans. Inf. Theory. **56**(12), 5930–5942 (2010)
22. Teixeira, A., Matos, A., Antunes, L.: Conditional Rényi entropies. IEEE Trans. Inf. Theory. **58**(7), 4273–4277 (2012)
23. Zografos, K., Nadarajah, S.: Survival exponential entropies. IEEE Trans. Inf. Theory. **51**(3), 1239–1246 (2005)
24. Viola, P., Wells III, W.M.: Alignment by maximization of mutual information. Int. J. Comput. Vis. **24**(2), 137–154 (1997)
25. Rusek, F., Lozano, A., Jindal, N.: Mutual information of IID complex Gaussian signals on block Rayleigh-faded channels. IEEE Trans. Inf. Theory. **58**(1), 331–340 (2012)
26. Boer, P., Kroese, D., Mannor, S., Rubinstein, R.: A tutorial on the cross-entropy method. Ann. Oper. Res. **134**(1), 19–67 (2005)
27. An, S., Yang, S., Ho, S.L., et al.: An improved cross-entropy method applied to inverse problems. IEEE Trans. Magn. **48**(2), 327–330 (2012)
28. Carvalho, L.M., González-Fernández, R.A., Leite da Silva, A.M., et al.: Simplified cross-entropy based approach for generating capacity reliability assessment. IEEE Trans. Power Syst. **28**(2), 1609–1616 (2013)
29. Li, X., Liu, B.: Maximum entropy principle for fuzzy variables. Int. J. Uncert. Fuzz. Knowl.-Based Syst. **15**(2), 43–52 (2007)
30. Chen, X., Dai, W.: Maximum entropy principle for uncertain variables. Int. J. Fuzz. Syst. **13**(3), 232–236 (2011)
31. Amari, S.I.: Natural gradient works efficiently in learning. Neural Comput. **10**(2), 251–276 (1998)
32. Rao, C.R.: Information and the accuracy attainable in the estimation of statistical parameters. Bull. Calcutta Math. Soc. **37**, 81–91 (1945)
33. Carter, K.M., Raich, R., Finn, W.G., et al.: FINE: fisher information nonparametric embedding. IEEE Trans. Pattern Anal. Mach. Intell. **31**(11), 2093–2098 (2009)
34. Efron, B.: Defining the curvature of a statistical problem (with applications to second order efficiency). Ann. Stat. **3**(6), 1189–1242 (1975)
35. Chentsov, N.N.: Statistical Decision Rules and Optimal Inference. American Mathematical Society, Rhode Island (1982)
36. Amari, S.I., Nagaoka, H.: Methods of Information Geometry. Oxford University Press, New York (2000)

37. Jamshidi, M.: System of Systems Engineering: Innovations for the 21st Century. John Wiley & Sons, Hoboken (2009)
38. Zaliwski, A.S.: Information-is it subjective or objective? Triple C Commun. Cap. Crit. **9**(1), 77–92 (2011)
39. Popper, K.R.: Objective Knowledge An Evolutionary Approach. Clarendon Press, Oxford (1991)
40. Steucke, M.: Marxism and Cybernetics. Berlin Institute of Technology, Berlin (1976)
41. Meriam, H.L.: Engineering Mechanics, Dynamics, vol. 2, 4th edn. John Wiley & Sons, New York (1979)
42. Xu, J., Wang, S., Liu, Z., Wang, Y.: Objective information theory exemplified in air traffic control system. Chin. J. Electron. **30**(4), 743–751 (2021)
43. Xu, J., Liu, Z., Wang, S., et al.: Foundations and applications of information systems dynamics. Engineering. **4**, 18 (2022). https://doi.org/10.1016/j.eng.2022.04.018
44. Xu, J.F., Tang, T., Ma, X.F., Xu, B., Shen, Y.L., Qiao, Y.J.: Objective information theory: a sextuple model and 9 kinds of metrics. Arxiv:1308.3372v1.
45. Xu, J., Sun, F., Chen, Q.: Introduction to Smart Court System Engineering (in Chinese). People's Court Press, Beijing (2021)
46. Gleick, J.: The Information: A History, A Theory, A Flood. Vintage, New York (2011)
47. Yan, X.S.: Information science: its past, present and future. Information. **2**(3), 510–527 (2011)

Chapter 2
Recognizing Objective Information

Abstract To understand the importance and necessity of studying objective information, in this chapter, it will first analyzes the similarities and dissimilarities
between objective information and subjective knowledge, then introduces the
basic forms of information, and finally gives the role of objective information.

Keywords Classifying objective information · Characterizing objective
information · Roles of objective information

2.1 Classifying Objective Information

Information could be classified in many ways. However, when it comes to studying
basic information science problems, nothing is more suitable than classifying them
into three basic types: nature information, behavior information, and media
information.

2.1.1 Nature Information

Nature information is the first basic form of objective information, directly magni-
fying the motion states of matter and energy in the objective world. The sun, the
moon and the stars, the rivers and mountains, the cities and streets, and the villages
and fields display nature information at every moment. So do the tender buds on the
trees in spring, the red leaves on the hill in autumn, the white hair on the head of the
elderly, as well as the fit body of the young reflected in the mirror. From this, we can
see that nature information acquaints us with nature's spectaculars in the most direct
manner. Its main features are as follows:

- The subjects of nature information are objects in the objective world, such as
  geographical and astronomical phenomena, architecture and artifacts, and animals and plants. Though there also exists the complicated subjective world for
  human beings, nature information only reflects external images.

J. Xu et al., *Objective Information Theory*, SpringerBriefs in Computer Science,
https://doi.org/10.1007/978-981-19-9929-1_2
19

- Nature information is time-variant. Landscapes may remain the same for a long time macroscopically but are constantly changing microscopically.
- Objective information could be reflected through both the subject itself and other carriers. The lofty mountains can display their magnificence to the climbers directly. They can also get reflected through other carriers such as water and air in reflections on the water or mirages.

2.1.2 Behavior Information

Behavior information is the second basic form of objective information. It is the indirect reflection of the effects of consciousness and mentalities in the subjective world upon matter and energy in the objective world. Human beings display their state of mood through expressions or languages by laughing and raging. Birds express their longing for survival and courtship through body gestures and sound by flipping and tweeting. Elephants linger around their deceased mate for a long time to show their deep sorrow. All these indicate that behavior information indirectly reflects consciousness and mentalities in the subjective world of human beings and other living creatures through movements, expressions, language, and sound. Its main features are as follows:

- The subjects of behavior information are consciousnesses and mentalities in the subjective world, such as instincts, desires, judgments, and decisions of human beings, animals, and even some plants and microorganisms.
- Behavior information is also time-variant. As subjective consciousness is complicated and constantly changing, the behaviors under its control would certainly exhibit different forms at different times.
- Behavior information could only be reflected indirectly through carriers like a body, sound, tools, and through the subject itself in the form of subjective status.

In the view of the author of this thesis: though devices attempting to peep at the subjective world of human beings, such as lie detectors, have been in existence for over a hundred years, the subjective world of living creatures would never be directly exposed however developed the technology is because the subjective and objective worlds belong to two entirely different categories. It is this fact that makes the existence and development of the world more intriguing.

2.1.3 Media Information

Media information is the third basic form of objective information. It refers to the images stored in the form of matter and energy after collecting, transmission, and processing of nature and behavior information. A large number of social news, figure commentaries, and encyclopedic knowledge recorded in newspapers, journals, and

Table 2.1 Basic forms, connotations and characteristics of objective information

Type	Connotation	Subject	Temporal characteristics	Carrier	Examples
Nature information	Direct reflection of the motion states of objects in the objective world	Objects in the objective world	Changing with time	The subjects themselves or other carriers	Landscapes, city scenarios and body figures
Behavior information	Indirect reflection of the effects of consciousness and mentalities in the subjective world on the objective world	Consciousness and mentalities in the subjective world	Changing with time	Other carriers except the subjects	Expressions, languages and voices of human beings as well as the body movements and tweeting of animals
Media information	The stored projection images of nature and behavior information	Objects in the objective world as well as consciousness and mentalities in the subjective world	Not changing with time	Other carriers except the subjects	Database, printed books and pictures, audiovisual materials

books is a kind of media information available for repeated reading. Audio and video broadcasts over the radio, film, and TV are media information available for repeated listening and watching. The huge amount of various data codes stored on Internet servers worldwide is also a form of media information capable of presenting or supporting the running of all kinds of information systems for their users. Media information records or copies all kinds of nature and behavior information, indirectly presenting the motion states of objects in the subjective and objective world in an enduring manner. It has the following features:

- The subjects of media information could be both objects in the objective world and consciousnesses and mentalities in the subjective one.
- Media information is stable in time, making it easy for users to repeat experiencing and processing.
- Media information can only reflect the motion and changing states of subjects through carriers like paper, bamboo slips, stones, disks, circuits, and screens.

Table 2.1 summaries the basic types of objective information as well as their corresponding connotations and characteristics. It illustrates the typical characteristics of the three kinds of information, i.e., nature, behavior, and media information, in terms of their different noumenon, State Sets, Carriers, and Times.

Objective information is quite inclusive. In terms of space, we could see starlight from over 100 light-years away and feel it as near as our heartbeat. In terms of time, we could observe something as ancient as the microwave background radiation left after the Big Bang and see something as recent as the scenery that comes in sight upon opening our eyes. In terms of size, it includes the macroscopic as the picture of the whole universe and as microscopic as the movement traces of basic particles in the high energy accelerator. In terms of form, there are both natural scenes familiar to us and data coding stored in various forms of media. Therefore, objective information pervades all living creatures and the vast universe in different forms. We could conduct classified researches on it from multiple perspectives.

Firstly, objective information contains specific content. Bright sunshine and roaring waves belong to nature information. Happy smiles and angry reproaches indicate emotional information. Election debates on TV and newspaper news about leaders reflect political information. Stock prices on the screen and the financial statements of enterprises show economic information. Delicate pictures in a museum and beautiful melodies in the concert represent artistic information. All these kinds of information differ from each other in content, which is where the value and significance of objective information lie.

Secondly, objective information is time-related. Lofty mountains and ancient architectures display their magnificence in an enduring manner. The rising and setting of the sun and the ebb and flow of the tide reflect the periodically changing pattern of nature. Shooting stars flashing through the sky and athletes passing the finishing line leave only a transient impression on us. All these show that objective information can be enduring, intermittent and transient in terms of time. Besides, as objective information comes into existence at different times, their emergence sequence can also serve as an important criterion for information classification. Information of the past is different from that of the present.

Besides, objective information has various carriers. The disposition, shape, color, temperature, and volume of matter could all bear different information. Therefore, matter itself is an important direct carrier of objective information. Meanwhile, as light shows the color of matter, sound reflects the motion state, electric current indicates the movement of an electric charge, the magnetic field shows the geographical position, and force reflects the interaction between matter. All of them are indirect carriers of objective information.

2.2 Characterizing Objective Information

Objective information is quite inclusive. In terms of space, we could see starlight from over 100 light-years away and feel it as near as our heartbeat. In terms of time, we could observe something as ancient as the microwave background radiation left after the Big Bang and see something as recent as the scenery that comes in sight upon opening our eyes. In terms of size, it includes the macroscopic as the picture of the whole universe and as microscopic as the movement traces of basic particles in the high energy accelerator. In terms of form, there are both natural scenes familiar to us and data coding stored in various forms of media. Therefore, objective information pervades all living creatures and the vast universe in different forms. We could conduct classified researches on it from multiple perspectives.

2.2.1 Scene Features

Objective information contains specific content. Bright sunshine and roaring waves belong to nature information. Happy smiles and angry reproaches indicate emotional information. Election debates on TV and newspaper news about leaders reflect political information. Stock prices on the screen and the financial statements of enterprises show economic information. Delicate pictures in a museum and beautiful melodies in the concert represent artistic information. All these kinds of information differ from each other in content, which is where the value and significance of objective information lie.

2.2.2 Temporal Features

Objective information is time-related. Lofty mountains and ancient architectures display their magnificence in an enduring manner. The rising and setting of the sun and the ebb and flow of the tide reflect the periodically changing pattern of nature. Shooting stars flashing through the sky and athletes passing the finishing line leave only a transient impression on us. All these show that objective information can be enduring, intermittent and transient in terms of time. Besides, as objective information comes into existence at different times, their emergence sequence can also serve as an important criterion for information classification. Information of the past is different from that of the present.

2.2.3 Carrier Features

Objective information has various carriers. The disposition, shape, color, temperature, and volume of matter could all bear different information. Therefore, matter itself is an important direct carrier of objective information. Meanwhile, as light shows the color of matter, sound reflects the motion state, electric current indicates the movement of an electric charge, the magnetic field shows the geographical position, and force reflects the interaction between matter. All of them are indirect carriers of objective information.

2.2.4 Significance Analysis

Shannon Information Theory first studies the uncertainty metric of information in communication systems [1], implying that the significance of communication information lies in eliminating uncertainty, which is no doubt reasonable and feasible speculation for communication systems. Subsequent studies define information as the ability to cause changes [2] or the proportion of changes brought to the structural complexity [3], which expands the understanding of the significance of information but still follows the basic thought of Shannon Information Theory to a certain extent. We consider it neither appropriate nor adequate to simply apply the speculations suitable for communication information to objective information.

In terms of the cause of existence, nature information comes into being due to the law of motion in the objective world itself. As for behavior information, though part of it arises from the subjective wish to change or eliminate uncertainties in cognition, many contents, just like expressions of all kinds of emotion by animals, result from species instincts. Media information, which are projection images that record nature and behavior information mainly out of the need to store for replay, is closely related to eliminating and changing uncertainties. However, there are some parts like artistic products which come into existence for sensory and mental enjoyment. So the existence of lots of objective information is not determined by whether it can change or eliminate uncertainty or not.

Therefore, the significance of objective information is not confined to changing or eliminating uncertainties. It also lies in helping the receivers feel the actual existence of the objective and subjective world. In fact, according to studies on cosmic large-scale structure formation and microwave background radiation, it is estimated that only 4% of the cosmos has been perceived, the remaining 23% being dark matter and 73% being dark energy. Dark matter and energy are called "dark" because they cannot produce information perceivable to us, namely objective information.

2.3 Roles of Objective Information

Based on the understanding of the objectivity of information, a large amount of nature, behavior, and media information could change or eliminate uncertainties in specific objects' cognition. However, the beautiful sceneries outside our window, though not constantly changing our understanding of the view, enable us to feel the beauty of nature all the time. Scenes of beasts chasing prey on the African plains, though not constantly altering the observers' perception of wild animals, strongly impresses them with the ruthless law-of-the-jungle. The music of the Blue Danube played on digital sounders, though not always strengthening the listeners' comprehension of the waltz, reminds them of the composers' briskness and serenity at heart every time it is played. From these examples, it is easy to see that the specific effects of objective information mainly lie in acquainting the receivers of the spectaculars of nature instead of changing or eliminating uncertainties.

The degree of uncertainty that could be changed or eliminated by nature information, behavior information, or media information varies with different receivers, displaying the distinct feature of relativity. However, through these kinds of objective information, it is beyond doubt that receivers feel the existence of the world around them. This indicates that the scope of change caused by objective information is relative, but the fact that objective information can inspire all receivers' feelings is absolute.

Objective information offers the only way for us to perceive the world. It has great significance and various specific effects, summarized as enabling the receivers to perceive the present, get to know the past, and foresee the future.

2.3.1   Summarizing the History

Getting to know the past is an indirect yet steady effect of objective information on receivers. The annual rings of trees reflect their past growth in the form of nature information. Books and media provide media information that reflects what happened in history. People get to know developments from all ages through these in an indirect yet accessible manner. Through this effect of objective information, the past gets closely and amply correlated to the present.

2.3.2   Perceiving the Present

Perceiving the present is the most transient and most direct effect of objective information on receivers. What people see when they look out is what nature information is in their current view, and what they hear when they talk is the behavior information they are communicating. As the "present" becomes the "past" in the twinkling of an eye, the effect of apperceiving the present is a transient one.

2.3.3   Foreseeing the Future

Foreseeing the future is an important effect of objective information that is easily ignored. We can foresee the success or failure of a hunt by watching the speed of the hunters' and their prey. An information system could figure out the target's future location with reasonable accuracy by observing the target's motion in the past and present. All these exhibit the critical role played by objective information in foreseeing the future. Because of this effect, a mutually traceable relationship gets established among the past, the present, and the future.

The above analysis shows that objective information is the link connecting everything in the world. Without which the world that we live in would be a broken, isolated, and dark one. Thus, objective information is considered one of the three key elements comprising the objective world, equivalent to matter and energy. For such an important subject as objective information, it deserves great effort to study its connotations, the mathematical expressions of its composition, and the mathematical models of its metrics. Only after solving these problems can we further understand the scientific mechanism whereby objective information connects the world and the operation processes and evolution laws of information systems acquiring, transmitting, processing, storing, and applying information.

2.4 Chapter Summary

Information is the link that connects everything in the world. It becomes one of the three major elements that constitute the objective world, and is equivalent to matter and energy. There are issues of objective information, i.e. defining connotation, expressing composition, and metric system. By solving these issues, we can further understand the mechanism of objective information linking everything in the world and the operation and evolution of acquisition, transmission, processing, storage, and application of information in a complex system.

References

1. Shannon, C.E.: The mathematical theory of communication. Bell Syst. Tech. J. **27**(1), 379–423 (1948)
2. Zhong, Y.: Principles of Information Science. Beijing University of Posts and Telecommunications Press, Beijing (2002)
3. Burgin, M.: Theory of Information: Fundamentality, Diversity and Unification. World Scientific Publishing, Singapore (2010)

Chapter 3
Modelling Objective Information: Sextuple

Abstract In this chapter, the objective information will be depicted from the philosophical view, formal assumption, and mathematical model. It uses mathematical language to give a sextuple model of information, discusses the basic properties of information, makes the definition of information more rigorous and clearer, and analyzes information systems.

Keywords Objective information theory (OIT) · Sextuple model · Information model · Information system model

3.1 Definition and Model

The objective information theory (OIT) has its roots in the philosophical view that *information is the objective reflection of objects and their state of motion in the objective and subjective worlds*, as inspired by Wiener's triadic theory of matter, energy, and information [1–3]. The attached information carrier reflects the motion state of the body at a specific time set. The specific time set is the time when the information state occurs, and the motion state is the information state set. Thus, we propose an accurate definition and mathematical model of information.

Assume that O, S, and T are the objective world set, subjective world set, and time set respectively. O includes the basic objects in Popper's first world and third world. S includes the basic objects in Popper's second world. T is the duration of information action. The elements in O, S, and T can be either continuous or discrete, subject to the specific requirement of the universe of discourse. The denotations of symbols or expressions are given in the following Table 3.1.

Let I denote objective information, o denote noumena (i.e., objects that originate information in the real world), c denote carriers (i.e., objects that transmit and maintain information in the real world), T_h denote the occurrence time, and T_m denote the reflection time. The set of all information I is called an information space. o belongs to either an objective world or subjective world, mathematically $o \in 2^{O \cup S}$. c only belongs to an objective world, thus $c \in 2^O$. T_h and T_m are both in temporal domain, $T_h \in 2^T$ and $T_m \in 2^T$. When I is depicted in the context of o, T_h, f, c, T_m, g simultaneously, a *sextuple model* comes into being.

Table 3.1 The denotations of symbols or expressions

Symbols or expressions	Condition	Meaning
O	The elements in O can be either continuous or discrete, subject to the specific requirement of the universe of discourse	The objective world set, in which the elements are the basic objects in the objective physical or knowledge world
S	The elements in S can be either continuous or discrete, subject to the specific requirement of the universe of discourse	The subjective world set, in which the elements are the basic objects in the subjective world
T	The elements in T can be either continuous or discrete, subject to the specific requirement of the universe of discourse	The time set, which is the duration of information action
2^O	The measurable set on O	The same can be obtained, 2^S, $2^{O \cup S}$
o	$o \in 2^{O \cup S}$	The objects that originate information in the real world, referred to as noumenon
c	$c \in 2^O$	The objects that transmit and maintain information in the real world, referred to as carrier
T_h	$T_h \in 2^T$	Occurrence time
T_m	$T_m \in 2^T$	Reflection time
$f(o, T_h)$	Non-empty sets	The set of o on T_h, referred to as state set
$g(c, T_m)$	Non-empty sets	The set of c on T_m, referred to as reflection set
$\langle o, T_h, f, c, T_m, g \rangle$	$I = \langle o, T_h, f, c, T_m, g \rangle$	The information sextuple model, viz. the mathematical definition of objective information
$\mathfrak{T}$	$\mathfrak{T} = \{I_1, I_2, \cdots, I_n\}$	The set of all information, referred to as information space
σ	Determined by the universe of discourse	The degree of a specific measure space
$(O, 2^O, \sigma)$	A measure space from O	A measure space on O with respect to σ
Λ	The elements can be either continuous or discrete, subject to the specific requirement of the universe of discourse	The index set, whose members index members of another set
$|X|$	X can be either continuous or discrete subject to the specific requirement of the universe of discourse	The cardinality of some set X.

$$I = \langle o, T_h, f, c, T_m, g \rangle \tag{3.1}$$

Thus I is modeled mathematically as a full mapping from $f(o, T_h)$ to $g(c, T_m)$.

$$I : f(o, T_h) \to g(c, T_m) \tag{3.2}$$

where, a state set $f(o, T_h)$ of o on T_h, and a reflection set $g(c, T_m)$ of c on T_m are all non-empty. If I is the surjective mapping from $f(o, T_h)$ to $g(c, T_m)$, Eq. (3.2) can be rewritten as

$$I(f(o, T_h)) = g(c, T_m) \tag{3.3}$$

In the light of the sextuple model with mathematical information definition, we can realize the dual deconstruction of the subject, temporal domain, and form of the information, respectively. These deconstructions of information make it possible to conduct more profound and comprehensive investigations of information beyond Shannon information theory.

3.2   Model Properties

Based on the sextuple model, we can mathematically infer five primary properties of information: objectivity, restorability, transitivity, combinability, and relevance.

3.2.1   Objectivity

The world is material, and matter is in motion. The moving matter constitute an infinite objective world in space and time. Humans perceive the objective world through contact and observation. People are originally unknown to many things in the objective world, and the degree of unknown is uncertainty. They obtain information about a certain part of the objective world through perceptual means, which reduces the uncertainty and improves the degree of awareness.

In the sextuple model, the separation of o and c is the binary deconstruction of the subjects of information I. Based on the deconstruction, I can be reflected by mapping from $f(o, T_h)$ to $g(c, T_m)$. Herein, c belongs to the objective world, and I can be perceived through the objective world, which is also why the OIT is named after the objectivity of information.

Owing to the objectivity of information, people can collect, transmit, process, aggregate, and apply information using various technical means. In fact, the rapid development of emerging technologies, such as AI, brain-like systems, and brain–computer interfaces, is driven by advances that simulate the human mind and then transform humanity's subjective processes into objective information that can be processed by information systems. Therefore, we consider the OIT to plays a fundamental role in the analysis and research of information systems and technologies.

3.2.2 Restorability

Defined as a type of mathematical mapping, I may have an inverse mapping I^{-1}. If $g(c, T_m)$ is on of c, T_m can be reduced to the state $f(o, T_h)$ of o on T_h by I^{-1}, then we call I restorable. This is the restorability of information. Here, $f(o, T_h)$ is also called the reduction state of I. The mathematical inference is as following.

$I = \langle o, T_h, f, c, T_m, g \rangle$ is a surjective map of $f(o, T_h)$ onto $g(c, T_m)$ and is called injective if for any $o_\lambda \in o$, $T_{h\lambda} \in T_h$, $f_\lambda \in f$, $o_\mu \in o$, $T_{h\mu} \in T_h$, $f_\mu \in f$ with $f_\lambda(o_\lambda, T_{h\lambda}) \neq f_\mu(o_\mu, T_{h\mu})$, there holds

$$I(f_\lambda(o_\lambda, T_{h\lambda})) \neq I(f_\mu(o_\mu, T_{h\mu})).$$

If $I = \langle o, T_h, f, c, T_m, g \rangle$ is injective, then it is called invertible since it is surjective by definition. In this case, there exists an inverse map I^{-1} of I. That is, for any $c_\lambda \in c$, $T_{m\lambda} \in T_m$, $g_\lambda \in g$, there exists a unique set of $o_\lambda \in o$, $T_{h\lambda} \in T_h$, $f_\lambda \in f$, s.t.

$$I^{-1}(g_\lambda(c_\lambda, T_{m\lambda})) = f_\lambda(o_\lambda, T_{h\lambda}).$$

This means that

$$I^{-1}(g(c, T_m)) = f(o, T_h).$$

For the invertible information $I = \langle o, T_h, f, c, T_m, g \rangle$, $g(c, T_m)$ of c on T_m can be reduced to the state $f(o, T_h)$ of o on T_h by I^{-1}, and have I restorable and $f(o, T_h)$ the reduction state of I.

Moreover, if there is a mapping J such that $J(g(c, T_m)) = \tilde{f}(\tilde{o}, \tilde{T}_h)$, where $\tilde{o}$ is referred to as reflection noumena ($\tilde{o} \in 2^{O \cup S}$), $\tilde{T}_h$ is referred to as reflection occurrence time ($\tilde{T}_h \in 2^T$), and $\tilde{f}(\tilde{o}, \tilde{T}_h)$ is a certain state set of $\tilde{o}$ on $\tilde{T}_h$, then J is called a reflection of I, and $\tilde{f}(\tilde{o}, \tilde{T}_h)$ is the reflection state of I based on J. When $J = I^{-1}$, $\tilde{f}(\tilde{o}, \tilde{T}_h)$ is the reduction state of I.

It should be noted that the isomorphism between the state set and the reflection set of restorable information is of great significance. Through isomorphism, the same mathematical method can be applied to two different sets of information, that is, noumenon states and carrier states. The objects in these sets have the same attributes and operations. The proposition established for one set can be established for another. This facilitates the use of abundant mathematical theories to support extensive research in the field of information science.

3.2.3 Transitivity

Information I can be transmitted from o to c and from c to other c' that is the reflection of c, from T_h to T_m and from T_m to another reflection time $T_m{}'$ that is the reflection of T_m, and from $f(o, T_h)$ to $g(c, T_m)$ and from $g(c, T_m)$ to another reflection set $g'\left(c', T'_m\right)$ through the compound mapping $I'(I(f(o, T_h)))$; that is, via the transitivity of information.

Information $I = \langle o, T_h, f, c, T_m, g \rangle$ is a surjective map from $f(o, T_h)$ onto $g(c, T_m)$. If there exists the set c' in the objective world, the time set T'_m, the set $g'\left(c', T'_m\right)$ of all states of c' on T'_m, and a surjective map,

$$I' : g(c, T_m) \rightarrow g'\left(c', T'_m\right)$$

with

$$I'(g(c, T_m)) = I'(I(f(o, T_h))),$$

then

$$I \circ I' = \langle o, T_h, f, c', T_m{}', g' \rangle$$

is also an information, where the set $g'\left(c', T'_m\right)$ is denoted by g'. This is the transitivity of pieces of information.

It is reasonable to state that it is due to the transmissibility of information such that information movement in the collection, transmission, processing, convergence, and action links can be realized. In particular, serial information transmission is a common form of information movement in information systems, so it is significant to analyze the mechanism of a serial information transmission chain.

3.2.4 Compositionality

In $I = \langle o, T_h, f, c, T_m, g \rangle$, $f(o, T_h)$ and $g(c, T_m)$ are mathematical sets. Thus I can naturally be decomposed or combined into different new sets, that is, information has compositionality. The mathematical inference is followed.

For two pieces of information $I' = \langle o', T'_h, f', c', T'_m, g' \rangle$ and $I = \langle o, T_h, f, c, T_m, g \rangle$ with

$$o' \subseteq o, T'_h \subseteq T_h, f' \subseteq f, c' \subseteq c, T'_m \subseteq T_m, g' \subseteq g$$

if for any $o'_1 \in o', T'_{h1} \in T'_h, f'_1 \in f'$, thereholds

$$I'\left(f_1{}'\left(o_1{}', T'_{h1}\right)\right) = I\left(f_1{}'\left(o_1{}', T'_{h1}\right)\right)$$

then I' is called sub-information of I, denoted as $I' \subseteq I$. We also say that I' is in I.

If, moreover, there holds $f' \subset f$, then I' is called a proper sub-information of I, denoted as $I' \subset I$. We also say that I' is properly in I.

If $I' = \langle o', T'_h, f', c', T'_m, g' \rangle$ and $I'' = \langle o'', T''_h, f'', c'', T''_m, g'' \rangle$ are two pieces of proper sub-information of the information $I = \langle o, T_h, f, c, T_m, g \rangle$ with $o = o' \cup o''$, $T_h = T'_h \cup T''_h$, $f = f' \cup f''$, $c = c' \cup c''$, $T_m = T'_m \cup T''_m$, $g = g' \cup g''$, then I is said to be a combination of I' and I'', denoted as $I = I' \cup I''$.

Naturally, information I can be decomposed or combined into several new sets. The compositionality of information determines that information can be flexibly split and arbitrarily combined, which creates sufficient conditions for people to determine the objects of information processing according to actual needs.

3.2.5 Relevance

The relevance of information manifests itself in at least three ways. Firstly, for information $I = \langle o, T_h, f, c, T_m, g \rangle$, o and c, T_h and T_m, and $f(o, T_h)$ and $g(c, T_m)$ all come in pairs. As a surjective map of f(o, T_h) onto g(c, T_m), information I establishes a particular connection between o and c. In particular, the information transmission is an important embodiment of information relevance, in which things are bridged together. Thus, people usually state that information is a bridge that connects things. Secondly, there may be connections between different pieces of information or the containment of one piece of information in another. Because various mutual relationships can exist between different pieces of information, which is a form of information correlation, people can utilize various analytical approaches to uncover the values of information. Thirdly, the most important form of information relevance is the internal relationships in a reduction state. Here, reductional information can completely retain the internal structure of the original information, which is an important prerequisite for accessing, processing, and analyzing the internal structure of information.

3.3 The Sextuple Model of Information System

An information system is a human-computer integrated system for processing information flow, which is composed of computer hardware, network and communication equipment, computer software, information resources, information users, and rules and regulations. Processes such as control provide information that meets user requirements and has corresponding metrics.

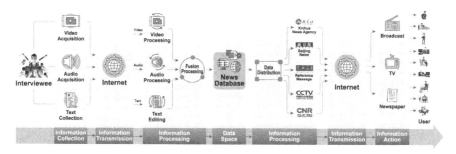

Fig. 3.1 Information flows during the news gathering and release process

The information system to manage and use information has become an integral element of the social system. Numerous information systems have changed the way people live and work. In modern information systems, information integration reflects the static characteristics and dynamic changes of things, and it is necessary to solve fundamental theoretical problems in information science, such as the essence of information, measurement methods, model algorithms, and controllability of calculations.

Figure 3.1 visualizes the information flows in the news gathering and release process. This intuitive scenario can help us understand the sextuple model of information. In Fig. 3.1, the information collection link primarily collects the state information of the interviewees through video, audio, text, and other collection means. In addition, the information transmission link transmits the collected information to the corresponding processing system through the Internet and other wide area networks, and the information processing link performed video, audio, text, and mutual fusion processing to form various news materials. These news materials are gathered into a comprehensive news database to support extensive access and application. Then, in the information processing link, news information with richer content and forms is distributed and arranged to satisfy the publishing conditions. Through the information transmission link, all types of media news information are then transmitted to various information terminals over the Internet. Finally, in the information action link, all kinds of terminal devices display the corresponding news information to different audiences or readers in a variety of formats.

According to the analysis of information space framework, the entire news gathering and release process includes seven important links, where the information in each link has six elements, i.e., noumenon, occurrence time, state set, carrier, reflection time, and reflection set. Table 3.2 shows the specific content. Note that the information noumenon and carrier at each link in Table 3.2 differ. In particularly, the noumenon, occurrence time, and state set of the next link are the carrier, reflection time, and reflection set of the previous link, respectively, which reflects the concept of information flow (an important characteristic of information transmission). In addition, the news information itself reflects the subjective and objective state of the interviewee; thus, the noumenon and state of all links can be understood as the

Table 3.2 Information elements in main links of news gathering and release process

Links in information systems	Noumenon (o)	Occurrence time (T_h)	State set (f)	Carrier (c)	Reflection time (T_m)	Reflection set (g)
Information collection (I_1)	Interviewees (o_1)	From the beginning to the end of the news interview (T_{h1})	Images, voice, and text of interviewees and the interview scene, as well as the subjective consciousness of the interviewees (f_1)	Video camera, camera, voice recorder, notebook, etc. (c_1)	From the beginning to the end of the news interview (T_{m1})	Image, voice, text, and other data and text collection of the interviewee and interview site (g_1)
Information transmission (I_2)	Video camera, camera, voice recorder, notebook, etc. (o_2)	From the beginning to the end of the news interview (T_{h2})	Image, voice, text, and other data and text collection of the interviewee and interview site (f_2)	Transmission links, e.g., the Internet (c_2)	From the beginning of news data transmission to the end of transmission (T_{m2})	Digital coding of images, voice, and text of the interviewees and interview site (g_2)
Information processing (I_3)	Transmission links such as the Internet (o_3)	From the beginning of news data transmission to the end of transmission (T_{h3})	Images, voice, text, and other digital contents of the interviewees and interview site (f_3)	Video processor, audio processor, codecs, news editing and clipping subsystem, etc. (c_3)	From the beginning of digital decoding to the completion of audio, video, text, and fusion processing (T_{m3})	News video, audio, text, and fusion material information (g_3)
Data space (I_4)	Video processor, audio processor, codec, news editing and clipping subsystem, etc. (o_4)	From the beginning of digital decoding to the completion of audio, video, text, and fusion processing (T_{h4})	News video, audio, text and fusion material information (f_4)	News database (c_4)	From entering news video, audio, text, and fusion information into the information database to deleting the corresponding content or disabling the database (T_{m4})	News video, audio, text, and fusion information (g_4)

Information processing (I_5)	News database (o_5)	From entering news video, audio, text, and fusion information into the information database to deleting the corresponding content or disabling the database (T_{h5})	News video, audio, text, and fusion information (f_5)	News media production subsystem (c_5)	From when news media began to accept video, audio, text, and fusion information to the completion of the production of publishing content editing (T_{m5})	News video, audio, and text content with broadcasting and publishing conditions (g_5)
Information transmission (I_6)	News media production subsystem (o_6)	From when news media began to accept video, audio, text, and fusion information to the completion of the production of publishing content editing (T_{h6})	News video, audio, and text content with broadcasting and publishing conditions (f_6)	Internet transmission link (c_6)	From the beginning to the end of the transmission of news articles (T_{m6})	Digital coding of news manuscript (g_6)
Information action (I_7)	Internet transmission link (o_7)	From the beginning to the end of the transmission of news articles (T_{h7})	Digital coding of news manuscript (f_7)	Television, radio, newspapers, mobile phones, etc. (c_7)	From the beginning to the end of the news broadcast and reading (T_{m7})	News video, audio, web pages, text, etc. (g_7)

subjective and objective content of the interviewee's image, voice, and text during the interview period, which is also a basic characteristic of information transmission.

3.4 Chapter Summary

This chapter defines the essence of information in the objective category, which not only conforms to the fundamental positioning of information as one of the three major components of the objective world, but also adapts to the operational requirements that information systems can handle objective and real information. It puts forward the mathematical expression and six aspects of information, i.e. the sextuple model, providing a unified, clear, convenient and feasible theory for all subsequent studies. Moreover, it demonstrates the objectivity, restorability, transmission, combination and relevance of information.

References

1. Xu, J., Wang, S., Liu, Z., Wang, Y.: Objective information theory exemplified in air traffic control system. Chin. J. Electron. **30**(4), 743–751 (2021)
2. Xu, J.F., Tang, T., Ma, X.F., Xu, B., Shen, Y.L., Qiao, Y.J.: Objective information theory: a sextuple model and 9 kinds of metrics. Arxiv:1308.3372v1.
3. Wiener, N.: Cybernetics: or the Control and Communication in the Animal and the Machine. The MIT Press, Cambridge (1961)

Chapter 4
Measuring Objective Information

Abstract In the context of the sextuple model, this chapter presents a metrics system with 11 indicators to measure objective information. Under the measurement, potential, and features of the set, each indicator is mathematical explored from the methodological foundations, specific definitions, and related propositions for quantitative information analysis and information systems applications.

Keywords Objective information theory (OIT) · Information measurement · Metric system on on information · Metric system on on information system

4.1 Motivations to Measure Information

The philosophy of objective information and the related sextuple model provide a powerful and flexible tool to derive various information metrics, which is inspired by both theoretical research and practical experience in the light of purpose and principle to measure information.

4.1.1 Prerequisite to Well Manage Information

Peter Drucker said "If you can't measure it, you can't manage it." A set of reasonable and feasible metrics to measure information is the prerequisite for managing and using information well [1]. Measurement is a quantitative description to describe the relationship between objects. Information measurement is one of the basic tasks of information comprehensive effectiveness evaluation and comprehensive integration. It has a positive significance for the effective use of information resources and guiding the scientific development of information system construction.

© The Author(s) 2023
J. Xu et al., *Objective Information Theory*, SpringerBriefs in Computer Science,
https://doi.org/10.1007/978-981-19-9929-1_4

4.1.2   Need to Comprehensively Master Information

There is a lack of a comprehensive of system for information metrics. To the best of our knowledge, Shannon information entropy is the only widely adopted information metric [2]. However, because information systems have evolved into different functionalities with complex structures far beyond those of communications, metrics based on entropy cannot comprehensively measure the complex dynamics of various information systems. Although other studies on the measurement of information exist, they lack for strict mathematical definitions and being systemic [3], making it difficult to establish an essential, basic reference framework for studying information mechanisms.

4.1.3   Requirement to Thoroughly Analyze Information Systems

There has been a lack of a thorough analysis of the efficacies of information systems. A dynamic mechanism describes how the target objects affect each other in a specific field. For example, in Newtonian mechanics, the efficiencies of speed, energy, and power were measured and analyzed to establish the theoretical system of mechanical dynamics. This methodology has also been applied in other fields. However, although information is pervasive in everyday life, there is a lack of a systematic approach to measuring and analyzing different efficacies of information systems. It is clear that only by establishing a complete analytical system of information efficacy can we accurately analyze the dynamic patterns in complex large-scale information systems.

4.1.4   Criteria to Measure Information

The information sextuple model depicts information with noumenon, state occurrence time, state set, carrier, reflection time, and reflection set, i.e. $I = \langle o, T_h, f, c, T_m, g \rangle$. To guide and regulate the derivation of information metrics, we should have come up with the following criteria.

- Traceability. The metrics are mathematically defined and derived from the sextuple model. It determines the specific definitions and mathematical expressions of various metrics according to the definition model of information.
- Completeness. The metrics are systematically defined and closely related to the value of the objective information. It forms a complete metric system which is closely related to its value according to the practical connotation of information.

- Generality. The metrics should be applicable to different information systems, such as information acquisition, transmission, processing, action, and their combinations, rather than being limited to a specific system. It forms metric definitions based on various categories of information which is universally applicable to any information systems.
- Practicability. The metrics should be able to guide the design, implementation, and analysis of practical information systems. It forms a practical and workable metric system that could guide the analysis and research of information systems according to the requirements.
- Openness. Owing to the characteristics of information, the metrics should continually evolve to match the needs of theoretical research and engineering applications. It forms a developing metric system that can supervise more and more complex information systems with newer and newer requirements.

To address these fundamental challenges, OIT takes information as the reflection of things and their movement states in the objective world and subjective world. It simplifies the concept of information from a general arbitrary idea to an objective concept in the real world, defining information as a mathematical mapping from objects in the real world to objects in information space. Based on the above principles, we will define 11 indicators for the metric system of information under the sextuple model. And the relevant basic propositions are also drawn from the set property such as metric, potential, and distance.

4.2   Metric System on Information

The metric system of objective information mainly includes 11 indicators: volume, delay, scope, granularity, variety, duration, sampling rate, aggregation, coverage, distortion, and mismatch (see Table 4.1). In Table 4.1, all of these indicators are defined and inferred with basic mathematical tools, such as set and measure, which allows them to accommodate classical information theories. For example, Shannon information entropy is a special case of the volume to measure the capacity of a communication system that transmits messages. In fact, for each metric indicator, a corresponding example can be found in classical or common information theories.

4.2.1   Volume

The value of information is closely related to its inherent containability, which is reflected by the required volume for the carrier. When other conditions are the same, the smaller the required volume is, the higher the information value is; and conversely, the lower the value is. So information may be measured by the volume.

Table 4.1 Classical theories of information science corresponding to different metrics

Metrics	Classical/common theories	Basic inference
Volume	Shannon information entropy	The minimum reducible volume of random event information is its information entropy
Delay	Whole and partial delay principle	The overall delay of serial information transmission is equal to the sum of the delays of each link
Scope	Radar equation [4]	The extent of radar detection information is directly proportional to the square root of transmitting power, antenna aperture, and antenna gain, and inversely proportional to the square root of detection sensitivity
Granularity	Rayleigh criterion for optical imaging [5]	The granularity of optical imaging information is proportional to the wavelength of light and inversely proportional to the width of the sampling pore
Variety	Invariance principle of reducible information type [6]	Reducible information can keep the type of information unchanged
Duration	Average duration of continuous information monitoring	The average time of information collection of the continuous monitoring system is equal to the mean time between failures of the system
Sampling rate	Nyquist's sampling theorem [7]	The lowest reducible sampling rate of the periodic function information is equal to half of its frequency
Aggregation	Invariance principle of aggregation degree of reducible information	Reducible information can keep the aggregation degree of the information unchanged
Coverage	Metcalfe's law [8]	The value of a network system is equal to the product of the maximum scope and the maximum coverage of all contained information
Distortion	Kalman's filtering principle [9]	A minimum distortion estimation method for linear systems with known metric variances
Mismatch	Average search length principle [10]	The shortest search path for minimum mismatch information in a finite set of information

Let $g(O \times T)$ be the set of state sets, which contains $g(c, T_m)$ on the objective world and temporal domain, and $(g(O \times T), 2^{g(O \times T)}, \sigma)$ be a measure space, where σ is a measure for the space. Then, the volume of information I relative to measure σ (viz. volume$_\sigma(I)$) is the measure $\sigma(g(c, T_m))$ of $g(c, T_m)$, which is expressed as follows:

$$\text{volume}_\sigma(I) = \sigma(g(c, T_m)) \tag{4.1}$$

In information systems, the volume of information is usually measured in bits, which is the most understandable information metric. In practice, the measure σ of $(g-(O \times T), 2^{g(O \times T)}, \sigma)$ for a specific task is determined by the universe of discourse. Therefore, the volume metric defined here is in a general form, but can be defined differently according to the practical needs. The metrics defined in the reminder of this study follow the same principle when applied in practice.

Volume is one of the most familiar and applied information metrics. Almost all information resources in the form of files in information systems use volume as a typical metric. Many information technologies have been developed in response to the need to keep the substantive content unchanged and minimize the information volume of the files. Data compression is one of them. Many classical information principles are related to the volume metric, and it is not difficult to prove that the minimum restorable volume of information of random events is the Shannon information entropy.

4.2.2 Delay

The value of information I is related to its timeliness, embodied in the delay between reflection time and occurrence time. Generally, when other conditions are the same, the shorter the delay is, the higher the information value is; and conversely, the lower the value is. So I may be measured by the delay.

Delay reflects the speed of the carrier response to the state of noumena. Therefore, the delay of information I (viz. delay(I)) is the difference between the supremum of its reflection time ($\sup T_m$) and the supremum of its occurrence time ($\sup T_h$), which is expressed as follows:

$$\text{delay}(I) = \sup T_m - \sup T_h \tag{4.2}$$

It is should be noted that this definition of delay allows for both positive and negative values. In particular, when $\sup T_m < \sup T_h$, delay(I) < 0. This represents the prediction of the future states by the carrier prior to the occurrence time T_h of the state for noumena. For example, the motion of targeted objects and the occurrence of events of interest can be predicted in information systems.

Actually, delay is also one of the most concerned information metrics. In fact, it will be insignificant for most information if its delay is too large. For example, if the delay of a weather forecasting information is positive, indicating that the carrier's reflection time is later than the actual weather occurrence time in the relevant region, the information of weather forecasting loses the significance of forecast. Therefore, people develop high-speed communication and high-performance computing technologies often with the purpose of reducing the delay metric of information. It is not difficult to prove that the total delay of serial information transmission is equal to the sum of information delays of each link in an information system.

4.2.3 Scope

Information is the objective reflection of noumenon, and its value is related to the noumenon scope. When other conditions are the same, the wider the noumenon scope is, the higher the information value is; and conversely, the lower the value is. So information can be measured by scope (coverage, extensity).

Let $(O \cup S, 2^{O \cup S}, \sigma)$ be the measure space over $O \cup S$. Let σ be some measure on $(O \cup S)$. According to the definitions of O and S, noumena o are elements of O and S, that is, $o \in 2^{O \cup S}$. Then, the scope of information I relative to measure σ (viz. $\text{scope}_\sigma(I)$) is the measure $\sigma(o)$ of o, which is defined as follows:

$$\text{scope}_\sigma(I) = \sigma(o) \tag{4.3}$$

The scope indicator reflects the extent of information noumena or information content, and is also an information metric that is highly valued by people. The Chinese idiom of "Climbing higher and looking farther" refers to the fact that a person can get a greater scope of visual field information when he/she climbs higher. Telescopes, radar and other detection tools are also designed to enable users to obtain a greater scope of information. It is not difficult to prove that the radar equation reveals the positive and negative proportional relationship between the scope of detection information and radar transmission power, antenna aperture, antenna gain and detection sensitivity.

4.2.4 Granularity

The value of information is directly related to the granularity of the noumenon it reflects. The granularity indicates the degree of coarseness of the particles into which the noumenon can be decomposed. When other conditions are the same, the finer the particles are, the higher the information value is; and conversely, the lower the value is. So information could be measured by granularity (detailedness).

For a pair of information I and I', if I' is proper sub-information of I and there is no other proper sub-information I'' of I such that $I'' \subset I'$, then I' is called the atomic information of I. Here, let $(O \cup S, 2^{O \cup S}, \sigma)$ be a measure space, and let σ be some measure on the set $(O \cup S)$. The set of all atomic information in information I is denoted as $A = \{I_\lambda = \langle o_\lambda, T_{h\lambda}, f_\lambda, c_\lambda, T_{m\lambda}, g_\lambda \rangle\}_{\lambda \in \Lambda}$, where Λ is an index set and λ is an index. In this case, let μ be the measure of the index set Λ and $\mu(\Lambda) \neq 0$. Then, the granularity of information I relative to measure σ (viz. $\text{granularity}_\sigma(I)$) is the ratio of the integral of all atomic noumenon information measures in A to the measure μ of index set Λ, which is expressed as follows:

$$\text{granularity}_\sigma(I) = \frac{\displaystyle\int_\Lambda \sigma(o_\lambda)\mathrm{d}\mu}{\mu(\Lambda)} \tag{4.4}$$

where it is most appropriate to take μ as the counting measure.

The granularity indicator reflects the degree of detail of information noumena or information content, and is also an indicator that people attach great importance to in their daily lives. With the development of display technology, the resolution of color TV is getting higher and higher, meaning that the TV image information is getting increasingly smaller granularity, which can provide viewers with an immersive watching experience. It is not difficult to prove that the Rayleigh criterion reflects the positive and negative proportional relationship between the granularity of optical imaging information and the light wavelength and sampling pore width, respectively.

4.2.5 Variety

For information I, let R be an equivalence relation on the set of states $f(o, T_h)$, and the set of equivalence classes of the elements in $f(o, T_h)$ relative to R is $[f(o, T_h)]_R$. Then, the variety of information I relative to R (viz. variety$_R(I)$) is the cardinality of set $[f(o, T_h)]_R$, which is expressed as follows:

$$\text{variety}_R(I) = \overline{[f(o, T_h)]_R} \tag{4.5}$$

For reducible information, the equivalence relation within state set can be transferred to reflection set. Therefore, the reflection set of the carrier can fully reflect the variety metric of information.

A rich variety of information provides a comprehensive understanding of what is of interest. Therefore, variety is an important indicator for measuring information. For example, when people have access to text, picture, audio and video information of the same object of interest, the variety of the whole information is increased, which thus enables them to know the object more comprehensively and deeply. Restorability is an extremely important property of information. It is not difficult to prove that the restorable information can maintain the invariance of the variety indicator.

4.2.6 Duration

The value of information is related to the duration of the noumenon it reflects. The duration indicates the density and span of occurrence time. When other conditions are the same, the higher the density is and the longer the span is, the higher the information value is. Conversely, the lower the value is. So information could be measured by the duration (sustainability).

The duration of information I (viz. duration(I)) is the difference between the supremum and infimum of T_h, which is expressed as follows:

$$\text{duration}(I) = \sup T_h - \inf T_h \qquad (4.6)$$

where $\inf T_h$ is the infimum of the occurrence time T_h.

The duration indicator reflects the time span of information and is certainly an important indicator for measuring information. Manufacturers of monitoring equipment are always looking for ways to extend the stable working time of their products in order to meet the requirements of users to constantly increasing the information duration indicator. It is not difficult to prove that the average duration of information collected by a continuous monitoring system is equal to its mean time between failures (MTBF).

4.2.7   Sample Rate

For information I, if $\inf T_h \neq \sup T_h$, let $\{U_\lambda\}_{\lambda \in \Lambda}$ be a family of pairwise disjoint connected sets that satisfy the following: for any $\lambda \in \Lambda$, there are $U_\lambda \subseteq [\inf T_h, \ \sup T_h]$, and $T_h \cap U_\lambda = \varnothing$. Then, the sampling rate of information I (viz. sampling _ rate(I)) is simply the ratio of the cardinality of Λ to the Lebesgue measure $|U|$ of $U = \bigcup_{\lambda \in \Lambda} U_\lambda$,

which is expressed as follows:

$$\text{sampling\_rate}(I) = \frac{\overline{\Lambda}}{|U|} \qquad (4.7)$$

Here, if $\inf T_h = \sup T_h$ or the Lebesgue measure of U is $|U| = 0$, then sampling _ rate $(I) = \infty$ is defined, which indicates that the state set of information I is completely continuous in time.

The sampling rate indicator reflects the sampling interval of information, which is closely related to the restorability of the information. It is not difficult to prove that Nyquist's sampling theorem reveals that the minimum restorable sampling rate of periodic function information is equal to half of its frequency, which is the essential requirement of information digitization.

4.2.8   Aggregation

The aggregation measures the similarity between different information, gathers similar information, separates dissimilar information, and divides the information into different clusters. The information similarity in the same cluster is the greatest, and the information dissimilarity between different clusters is the greatest. The aggregation starts from sample data, simplifies data through data modeling, and automatically clusters, which can be used as the basis for information classification.

For information I, if the cardinality of set $f(o, T_h)$ is $\overline{f(o, T_h)} \neq 0$, let $\mathfrak{R}$ be the set of relations between all elements on the state set $f(o, T_h)$. Then, the aggregation of I (viz. aggregation(I)) is the ratio of the cardinality of set $\mathfrak{R}$ to that of set $f(o, T_h)$, which is expressed as follows:

$$\text{aggregation}(I) = \frac{\overline{\mathfrak{R}}}{\overline{f(o, T_h)}} \tag{4.8}$$

The aggregation metric characterizes the distance between the elements of the state set $f(o, T_h)$ in the information space. In general, the closer the distance is between the elements of the state set $f(o, T_h)$, the higher the degree of aggregation and the higher the value of the information.

The aggregation indicator reflects the degree of relevance of information content. Data fusion technology exactly uses the relevance of information content for in-depth processing to optimize other information metrics and meet the requirements of users in many aspects. It is not difficult to prove that the restorable information can maintain the invariance of the degree of aggregation.

4.2.9   Coverage

The value of information is often related to its distribution, which is reflected by the coverage of the carrier. For some information, the wider the coverage is (within a certain extent), the higher the Information value is. For other information, the narrower the coverage is, the higher the value is. So, in any case, information could be measured by the coverage (distribution).

For information I and I', if there are inverse mappings I^{-1} and I'^{-1}, such that $I^{-1}(g(c, T_m)) = I'^{-1}(g'(c', T'_m)) = f(o, T_h)$, then information I and I' are called to be copies of each other. Here, let $\{I_\lambda = \langle o_\lambda, T_{h\lambda}, f_\lambda, c_\lambda, T_{m\lambda}, g_\lambda \rangle\}_{\lambda \in \Lambda}$ be a set containing information I and all of its copies. Then, the coverage of information I relative to some measure σ on a measurable set of c (viz. coverage$_\sigma(I)$) is the integral of all measures c_λ, which is expressed as follows:

$$\text{coverage}_\sigma(I) = \int_\Lambda \sigma(c_\lambda)\mathrm{d}\mu \tag{4.9}$$

The coverage indicator reflects the extent of distribution and knowledge of information content. Information encryption technology exactly adopts the approach to minimizing the coverage of information to the most extent in accordance with the right to know. Notwithstanding, the general online propaganda seeks to find ways to increase the coverage indicator of information. Therefore, the number of clicks and views has become a characteristic indicator to measure the value of a website in today's era, which is essentially the coverage of information. It is not difficult to prove that Metcalfe's law can also be expressed as the value of the network system is equal to the product of the maximum scope of information it can obtain and the maximum coverage of information it can distribute.

4.2.10   Distortion

As the mapping between noumenon state and carrier state, information should not be labeled true or false. According to the property of restorability, there always exists an inverse mapping of information in theory that could restore the actual state of information noumenon at the occurrence time. However, due to the complexity of the mapping process and the existence of subjective factors in the perception process, it is often impossible to acquire the exact inverse mapping of information. Therefore, only by deducing as far as possible can we get close to the actual state of noumenon at the occurrence time.

For information I and its reflection J, let the state set $f(o, T_h)$ and reflection state set $\tilde{f}(\tilde{o}, \tilde{T}_h)$ be elements in a distance space $\langle \mathcal{F}, d \rangle$, where $\mathcal{F}$ is the set of reflection sets and d is the distance on $\mathcal{F}$. Then, the distortion of reflection J of information I (viz. distortion$_J(I)$) is the distance between $\tilde{f}(\tilde{o}, \tilde{T}_h)$ and $f(o, T_h)$ in the distance space $\langle \mathcal{F}, d \rangle$, which is expressed as follows:

$$\text{distortion}_J(I) = d\left(f, \tilde{f}\right) \tag{4.10}$$

The distortion metric measures the degree of deviation between the reflection state and reduction state. The reflection state of information I is its reduction state if and only if the distortion$_J(I) = 0$.

Distortion is a negative indicator of the authenticity of information and is certainly one of the most concerned information metrics. It is hard to imagine that normal people need information that has lost its authenticity. Therefore, reducing errors by all means, that is, reducing information distortion, is one of the objectives for people to apply various technical means to process information since ancient times. It is not difficult to prove that Kalman filtering principle reveals the estimation method of the minimum information distortion for linear systems with known variance.

4.2.11 Mismatch

The value of information eventually depends on what degree it matches users' demand, embodied in the overall degree to which the various elements of information [11]. Generally speaking, the higher the overall degree is, the higher the information value is; conversely, the lower the value is. So information could be measured by mismatch (suitability).

Let information $I_0 = \langle o_0, T_{h0}, f_0, c_0, T_{m0}, g_0 \rangle$ be the target of information $I = \langle o, T_h, f, c, T_m, g \rangle$, let o_0 and o, T_{h0} and T_h, f_0 and f, c_0 and c, T_{m0} and T_m, and g_0 and g be elements in the sets $\mathcal{P}_o, \mathcal{P}_{T_h}, \mathcal{P}_f, \mathcal{P}_c, \mathcal{P}_{T_m}$, and $\mathcal{P}_g$, respectively, and let I_0 and I be elements in the distance space $\langle (\mathcal{P}_o, \mathcal{P}_{T_h}, \mathcal{P}_f, \mathcal{P}_c, \mathcal{P}_{T_m}, \mathcal{P}_g), d \rangle$. Then, the mismatch of information I to target information I_0 (viz. $\text{mismatch}_{I_0}(I)$) is the distance between I and I_0 in the distance space $\langle (\mathcal{P}_o, \mathcal{P}_{T_h}, \mathcal{P}_f, \mathcal{P}_c, \mathcal{P}_{T_m}, \mathcal{P}_g), d \rangle$, which can be expressed as follows:

$$\text{mismatch}_{I_0}(I) = d(I, I_0) \tag{4.11}$$

For the distortion and mismatch of information, we have not got the relationship between the measurements of the part and the whole, showing that neither the distortion nor mismatch would change along with the amount of information. This conforms to both common sense and the operation rules of information systems.

Mismatch is a negative indicator reflecting the degree to which information meets the requirements of users. It is the eternal goal of information systems to deliver the right content to the right object at the right time and place, which actually requires the use of various information technologies to continuously reduce the mismatch of all output information of information systems. It is not difficult to prove that the average search length principle reveals the shortest search path for information with minimum mismatch in a finite set of information.

4.3 Metric System on Information System

The metrics system on information can be further used to evaluate the effectiveness of complex information system, and the quality of informatization.

4.3.1 System of Systems

An system-of-systems (SoS) is a collection of task-oriented systems that offer more functionality and a greater performance than simply the sum of the constituent systems. With the ever-growing scales and complexities of information systems, it is becoming increasingly difficult for people to understand and grasp information systems, particularly SoS. Owing to the influence of various internal and external uncertainties, the dynamic behavior of these complex SoS may deviate from their original purpose, and unstable phenomena may appear. Moreover, in the construction and application of such large-scale SoS, an emphasis on order alone, while ignoring vitality, will lead to system rigidity, whereas an emphasis on vitality alone, while ignoring order, will lead to system chaos. Therefore, there is an urgent need for measuring the information during the process of the design, development, application, and evaluation of large-scale SoS.

4.3.2 Metric Effects and Efficacies of Information Systems

Any information system can be simplified as a basic process of information input, process, and output. The significance of information systems lies in their various efficacies. That is, the abilities of information systems to act on the input information and the effects expressed through the output information. In a large scale SoS, different efficacies are usually intertwined owing to complex information movements. Without a comprehensive analysis, reasonable deconstruction, and quantitative expression of these efficacies, it is difficult to deeply understand the inherent rules of the operation mechanism of information systems. Consequently, it is impossible to develop theoretical information systems dynamics (ISD) to guide the construction and development of large-scale SoS. Therefore, accurately and comprehensively measuring various efficacies of information systems is of decisive significance for an in-depth study on ISD.

Efficacy cannot be expressed quantitatively without certain metrics; thus, there must be an effective metric for a specific efficacy. The aforementioned 11 metrics can be used to measure various aspects of the effect on the input and output of information systems, which we refer to as the metric effect. It is therefore natural to apply these metrics to comprehensively and quantitatively describe and analyze the main efficacies of information systems. Specifically, there are 11 information system efficacies that can be established through 11 types of metric effects—namely, the volume, delay, scope, granularity, class, duration, sampling rate, aggregation, coverage, distortion, and mismatch efficacies.

- The volume is the most fundamental one that information systems act on information amongst various efficacies. In practice, each link of information collection, transmission, processing, data space and action can affect the volume efficacy by changing the capacity of the system. For example, the insufficient storage of information collection, data space and information action will lead to the reduction of the volume efficacy of information systems. The insufficient channel bandwidth of information transmission system will lead to discard part of the information, thus reducing the volume efficacy. Information processing also needs enough storage space to support, thus also affects the volume of information. Note that information processing systems can affect volume efficacy by the data compression processing, that is, the total information volume of whole system is increased by the decompression of some information.

- The delay is the ability of information systems to change the delay metric. In fact, all information flows and processing require a period of time, so each link of information collection, transmission, processing, data space and information action will certainly affect the delay metric. However, through the improvement of hardware or algorithms, each link can also achieve the lowest possible delay, so as to optimize the delay efficiency of the whole system. In particular, in the information processing link, the state set of the noumenon in the future can be predicted by the extrapolation algorithm in time dimension, which can actually reduce the delay metric of information and thus improve the delay efficiency of the information system.
- The scope characterizes the ability of information systems to change the scope metric of information noumena. In the information collection link, the scope metric of information acquisition is affected by the energy, distribution and other physical attributes of the acquisition equipment. For instance, the physical parameters such as antenna aperture, transmitter power, receiver sensitivity of radar determine the radar's detection range, viz. the scope of acquired information. The information processing link can also affect the scope effect of the output information due to the differences in the algorithms or the equipment. Note that although the information processing link does not directly involve the information noumena, it can also extend the scope of information noumena through the extrapolation algorithm in spatial dimension, thereby improving the scope effect of information. Data space, as the reflection of the real-world in information systems, certainly affects the scope effect of information by the integrity of the data model, database capacity and etc. Remarkably, the volume efficacy of information transmission step can also affect the scope effect of information, but in an indirect manner. Here, we can assume that the information transmission does not have the scope efficacy.
- The granularity is the ability of information systems to change the information granularity metric. Granularity metric characterizes the meticulousness of information noumena. In the information acquisition link, the granularity metric of information can be affected by the aperture area of the acquisition device, the number of sensors and other physical attributes. For instance, the number of photoelectric sensors integrated in the video information acquisition device determines the resolution or pixels of the video picture, which is the granularity efficacy of information acquisition. Information processing will also affect the granularity-effect of information due to the differences in the algorithms or the equipment. For instance, through interpolation algorithms in spatial dimension, it

is possible to optimize the granularity of information. Data space can also affect the granularity effect of information by factors such as the model integrity, granularity, and database capacity. Similar to the analysis of scope efficacy, the information transmission does not directly have the granularity efficacy on information.

- The variety is the ability of information systems to change the information variety metric, which characterizes the richness [12] of the state set types of information subjects. Each link in information space can affect the variety metric of information. The information acquisition and action can obtain and output different types of information owing to the differences in input and output methods. For example, microwave acquisition and audio acquisition devices can obtain different input information, and optical output and audio output devices can also produce different output information.

- The duration is the ability of information systems to change the information duration metric. Duration characterizes the time span of information continuity. Therefore, the duration of information collection directly determines the duration metric of information, and the duration of information processing also affects the duration metric of output information. Although in many cases, the duration of information transmission does not necessarily affect the duration metric of output information, there are some special cases that the duration of information transmission will directly affect the duration metric. For instance, the case of live broadcasting, usually occurs in radio and television. In general, information processing does not directly affect the duration metric of information, but by extrapolating, the state set of information can be expanded in time dimension, which actually affects the duration metric of information. Obviously, the storage capacity and structural design of the data space can directly affect the duration metric of information. Therefore, all links in information space have duration efficacy.

- The sampling rate is the ability of information systems to change the information sampling rate metric, which characterizes the occurrence density of the information state set in time. Obviously, the density of information collection directly determines the sampling rate metric of information. For instance, Nyquist sampling theorem shows that for periodic sine function curve, as long as the sampling rate is higher than half of its frequency, the original function curve can be restored by sampling information. Similarly, the frequency of information action can affect the intensity of the output information, viz. the sampling rate metric. In information transmission, if the bandwidth of the communication system is higher than the sampling rate of the input information, it will not affect the sampling rate of the output information, otherwise it will inevitably reduce the sampling rate. In general, information processing does not directly affect the sampling rate metric of information. However, through interpolation, the state set can be predicted in time. Thus, information processing can also affect the sampling-rate metric of information. The storage capacity and structure design of data space can directly affect the sampling rate metric of information. Therefore, each link in information space has sampling rate efficiency.

- The aggregation is the ability of information systems to change the aggregation metric, which characterizes the closeness of the elements in the information state set. Normally, information collection and transmission does not directly affect the information aggregation. Through the analysis, association and fusion of information processing, the internal pattern of information state set can be revealed, which improves the information aggregation metric. The internal structure and model design of data space can directly determine the aggregation metric of information. The information action, which is based on information processing and data space, certainly has the aggregation metric of information. Therefore, the information processing, data space and information action have the aggregation efficacy.
- The coverage is the ability of information systems to change the information coverage metric, which reflects the pervasiveness of information carrier and its copies. In general, information collection does not involve the formation of information copies, so it has not the coverage efficacy. Information action ultimately produces output information, and the scale of action directly affects the coverage metric of information. In information transmission, the distribution of communication networks determines the coverage of information, so information transmission has the coverage efficacy. Although information processing does not directly interact with users, the targeting or distribution processing determines the targets of information action, so it also affects the coverage metrics. Both the distributed structure design and the replica distribution range of data space are directly related to the coverage metric. Therefore, there are information transmission, processing, data space and information action that have the coverage efficacy.
- The distortion is the ability of information systems to change the information distortion metric. Obviously, most of information collection are physical or human-in-loop processes, which often produce errors due to various reasons, thus increases the distortion of information. Similarly, most information actions are also physical or human-in-loop processes, which can also affect the distortion metric of information. Information transmission can increase the distortion of information due to the limitation of communication bandwidth, error code, packet loss or other reasons. Information processing can increase the distortion of information due to computation errors, whereas the filtering, smoothing or other processing algorithms can reduce the distortion metric of information. Information representation and storage in the data space can also affect the distortion metric of information. Therefore, all links in information space have the distortion efficacy.
- The mismatch is the ability of information systems to change the information mismatch metric. The information mismatch metric reflects the degree of deviation to the needs of users. Note that all users concern the distortion metric. As each link in information space has distortion efficiency, it can be simply inferred that each link also has mismatch efficiency.

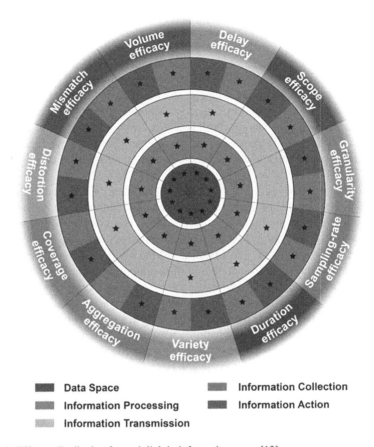

Legend:
- Data Space
- Information Processing
- Information Transmission
- Information Collection
- Information Action

Fig. 4.1 Efficacy distribution for each link in information space [13]

Figure 4.1 illustrates the information efficiency distribution across the information space. In the figure, the star symbol indicates the existence of the corresponding efficiencies, represented by the sectors, of some link. The collection and action of information are positioned in the same ring at the periphery, and are distinguished by two different shades of blue: The dark blue represents the information collection link, and the light blue represents the information action link. Therefore, the functionality and performance of an SoS can be deconstructed through the efficacy distribution, which provides a sufficient and quantitative basis for the design, analysis, testing, and integration of an SoS.

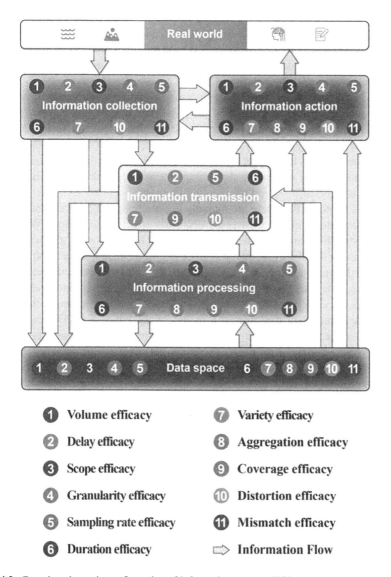

Fig. 4.2 Complete dynamic configuration of information systems [13]

4.3.3   Dynamic Configurations of Information Systems

In Fig. 4.2, the operating mechanism and efficacy distribution of various information links—that is, information collection, transmission, processing, storage, and action are presented, along with the possible information flows between the links; these are referred to as the integral dynamic configuration of an SoS. Information flow is the form and carrier of information movement in an SoS. In general, as long as information flow maintains its continuity, we can use the local metric effects at various links to analyze the global functionalities and performance of an entire SoS, which is the starting point to investigate ISD and the original intent of applying ISD to guide the planning, design, research and development, and integration of information systems.

In Fig. 4.2, each link in an SoS can affect the functionality and performance of an entire system. In general, the effects of the same class at each link can have mutual superposition or mutual restraint. For example, the delay effect at each link can be superimposed to form the delay effect of the entire SoS. In addition, the volume metric of the previous link forms the volume requirement for the subsequent link. If the requirement is not satisfied at the subsequent link, the volume efficiency of the entire SoS is affected.

It should be noted that there are mutual effects among the different metrics. For example, the volume effect impacts the distortion effect of the system. With insufficient volume, the elements in the reflection set will be abandoned, which will result in an increase in the distortion metric. The degree of mismatch reflects the degree to which the information output of the system deviates from the needs of specific users. The volume, delay, scope, granularity, duration, class, sampling rate, and aggregation metrics are closely related to the needs of specific users, meaning that any of these metrics can affect the mismatch metric of the entire SoS. For example, to control the range of information acquisition, the coverage metric must be adjusted according to the desires of the users. Therefore, the coverage metric is not related to the mismatch metric in a single direction. In addition, the distortion metric is not positively correlated with the mismatch metric. For example, in an encrypted information system, higher distortion results in lower mismatch for a specific user.

In engineering practices, users do not always need to apply the integral dynamic configuration of information systems. In many cases, some links of the SoS may not determine or affect the key efficacies of the entire SoS. In such cases, it is possible to limit the consideration of system designers to relatively minor links and form the simplified dynamic configurations for the information systems. Studying the mechanism of the efficacies with various configurations to reveal the inherent operating regularities of information systems provides a powerful means of guiding the planning and development of the large-scale SoS in engineering practices.

4.4 Chapter Summary

This chapter systematically establishes 11 efficiencies of measurement systems for information, defines the mathematical expression of each measurement from the basic model, and discusses the basic properties of each measurement, providing a theory for quantitative research and analysis of information operation and information system applications, and method basis.

References

1. Vigo, R.: Representational information: a new general notion and measure of information. Inf. Sci. **181**(21), 4847–4859 (2011)
2. Shannon, C.E.: The mathematical theory of communication. Bell Syst. Tech. J. **27**(1), 379–423 (1948)
3. Yan, X.S.: Information science: its past, present and future. Information. **2**(3), 510–527 (2011)
4. Skolnik, M.I.: Radar Handbook, 2nd edn. McGraw-Hill, New York (1990)
5. Lord Rayleigh, F.R.S.: Investigations in optics, with special reference to the spectroscope. Philos. Mag. **8**(49), 261–274 (1879)
6. Nyquist, H.: Certain factors affecting telegraph speed. J. Am. Ins. Elect. Eng. **43**(12), 1197–1198 (1924)
7. Lienig, J., Bruemmer, H.: Reliability analysis. In: Fundamentals of Electronic Systems Design. Springer, Berlin (2017)
8. Shapiro, C., Varian, H.R., Carl, S.: Information rules: a strategic guide to the network economy. Harvard Business Press, Boston (1998)
9. Kalman, R.: A new approach to linear filtering and predicted problems. J. Basic Eng. **82**, 35–45 (1960)
10. Flores, I., Madpis, G.: Average binary search length for dense ordered lists. Commun. ACM. **14**(9), 602–660 (1971)
11. Unnikrishnan, J., Huang, D., Meyn, S.P., et al.: Universal and composite hypothesis testing via mismatched divergence. IEEE Trans. Inf. Theory. **57**(3), 1587–1603 (2011)
12. Daft, R.L., Lengel, R.H.: Information richness: a new approach to managerial information processing and organization design. Manag. Sci. **32**(5), 554–571 (1986)
13. Xu, J., Liu, Z., Wang, S., et al.: Foundations and applications of information systems dynamics. Engineering. **4**, 18 (2022). https://doi.org/10.1016/j.eng.2022.04.018

Chapter 5
Exemplifying Objective Information: Air Traffic Control System

Abstract Air Traffic Control System (ATCS) is a large-scale information system that spreads all over the world and is widely used (Zhang et al., Modern Air Traffic Management (in Chinese). Beijing University of Aeronautics and Astronautics Press, Beijing, 2005). Although it cannot represent the entire information system, its structure, functional composition and application methods can already reflect many basic characteristics of today's information systems, especially large-scale information systems. In this chapter, OIT is applied to explain the behavior of ATCS for demonstrating the feasibility and practicality to investigate information systems.

Keywords Objective information theory (OIT) · Air traffic control system (ATCS) · Exemplification

5.1 The Air Traffic Control System (ATCS)

ATCS is the core system for implementing airspace management, ensuring flight safety and maintaining the order of air transport, and also an information system of colossal volume, great complexity and typical significance [1]. The navigation intelligence, dynamic meteorological information, flight rules and regulations as well as static materials that are acquired, processed or generated by ATCS are the sources of operation for the whole system [2]. Thereinto, the flight status, meteorological and geographical information are the variations of the objective world, while flight regulations are subjectively stipulated by men. Once being imported and documented, all this information will become the objective reflection of the related objects and their motion states in ATCS, supporting the operation and management of ATCS [3].

© The Author(s) 2023
J. Xu et al., *Objective Information Theory*, SpringerBriefs in Computer Science,
https://doi.org/10.1007/978-981-19-9929-1_5

5.2   The Sextuple of ATCS

For ATCS, its information set includes flight data, airport information, navigation and regional charts, national and international NOTAM, navigation chart information, route information, airport live weather reports, runway visual range, airport weather forecasts, significant weather alerts, weather images, air traffic control regulations, agreements with surrounding areas, procedures for handling special circumstances, airplane performance parameters and other data codes, etc. Table 5.1 characterizes the main elements of the aforesaid information in ATCS.

In Table 5.1, the noumenon of flight information include both objective objects, i.e. flights and other flying objects, and subjective consciousness of the pilots, since flight data reflects not only the motion parameters of flying objects, but also the pilots' operational intentions. Take the 9.11 attack for example, after the terrorists' hijacking of the plane, the most significant information in the air traffic control system is nothing but the subjective intention of the pilot, which is reflected through flight data. Thus, the state set of flight data contains not only the position, speed and direction of the flying object, but also subjective factors such as the pilot's operational intention. However, the reflection set only includes the motion parameters of the flying object, but not the subjective intention of the pilot.

The carriers of each information item are put into different subsystems of ATCS according to their features in retention and application. In fact, ATCS itself is the carrier of all these information items, while the subsystems in ATCS, such as communication gateway subsystem, information distribution subsystem and system data backup subsystem etc., may become the carriers of relevant information at the corresponding moments. For the sake of conciseness, many trivial details are omitted here.

The reflection time of all information items in Table 5.1 is "from acquisition & import to the outage of ATCS", because even when the aforesaid information items become outdated, they may still play a part in supporting and assisting the operation control in the future, and therefore, the advanced ATCS would save these information items in case of need.

In Table 5.1, the air traffic control regulations, the agreements with neighboring areas and the procedures for handling special circumstances etc. are all products of subjective will, but once issued, signed or stipulated, they will become important objective information stored in ATCS, supporting the air traffic control institutions and ATCS in the management and control of flying objects.

The sextuple model of OIT in ATCS indicates the specific components of an information item.

$$I = \langle o, T_h, f, c, T_m, g \rangle.$$

where, o, T_h, f, c, T_m, g denote the noumenon, state occurrence time, state set, carrier, reflection time and reflection set of information I in ATCS respectively. Table 5.1 indicates 16 information items in ATCS. From the third row on Table 5.1,

Table 5.1 The main elements of the information set in ATCS

No.	Information type (l)	Noumenon (o)	State occurrence time (T_h)	State set (f)	Carrier (c)	Reflection time (T_m)	Reflection set (g)
1	Flight data	Flights, other flying objects and the pilots' subjective consciousness	From taking off to landing	Parameters such as the position, speed and direction of the flying object, and the pilots' operational intension	Radar, secondary radar, and integrated information display subsystem etc.	From acquisition and import to the outage of ATCS	Parameters such as the position, speed and direction of the flying object
	(l_1)	(o_1)	(T_{h1})	(f_1)	(c_1)	(T_{m1})	(g_1)
2	Airport information	Relevant regional airports	From the last issuance to the latest renewal	Parameters such as reference point, runway, parking apron and communication facilities etc.	Data maintenance subsystem	From acquisition and import to the outage of ATCS	Parameters such as reference point, runway, parking apron and communication facilities etc.
	(l_2)	(o_2)	(T_{h2})	(f_2)	(c_2)	(T_{m2})	(g_2)
3	Navigation and regional charts	Navigation areas	From the last delimitation to the next renewal	Division coordinate data and images of airway, restricted area and prohibited area	Basic data processing subsystem	From acquisition and import to the outage of ATCS	Division coordinate data and images of airway, restricted area and prohibited area
	(l_3)	(o_3)	(T_{h3})	(f_3)	(c_3)	(T_{m3})	(g_3)
4	National and international NOTAM	Flights and other flying objects	From the issuance of announcement to the next renewal	Data on the time of the flight beginning and ending, the starting point and destination, and the flight route etc.	Basic data processing subsystem	From acquisition and import to the outage of ATCS	Data on the time of the flight beginning and ending, the starting point and destination, and the flight route etc.
	(l_4)	(o_4)	(T_{h4})	(f_4)	(c_4)	(T_{m4})	(g_4)
5	Navigation chart data	Airport and navigation areas			Data maintenance subsystem	From acquisition and	

(continued)

Table 5.1 (continued)

No.	Information type	Noumenon	State occurrence time	State set	Carrier	Reflection time	Reflection set
	(l_5)	(o_5)	From the last issuance to the latest renewal (T_{h5})	Images of the distribution of airports, airlines and special areas (f_5)	(c_5)	import to the outage of ATCS (T_{m5})	Images of the distribution of airports, airlines and special areas (g_5)
6	Route information (l_6)	Relevant regional routes (o_6)	From the last issuance to the latest renewal (T_{h6})	Data on the flight direction, flight altitude, capacity and obstacles etc. (f_6)	Data maintenance subsystem (c_6)	From acquisition and import to the outage of ATCS (T_{m6})	Data on the flight direction, flight altitude, capacity and obstacles etc. (g_6)
7	Airport live weather reports (l_7)	Weather conditions of the airport and nearby regions (o_7)	From a certain moment in the past to the present (T_{h7})	Images and data on the distribution and intensity of wind, cloud, rain, snow, fog and thunder (f_7)	Weather information query subsystem (c_7)	From acquisition and import to the outage of ATCS (T_{m7})	Images and data on the distribution and intensity of wind, cloud, rain, snow, fog and thunder (g_7)
8	Runway visual range (l_8)	Weather conditions of the runway (o_8)	From a certain moment in the past to the next renewal of weather forecast (T_{h8})	Parameters such as vertical visibility and horizontal visibility etc. (f_8)	Weather information query subsystem (c_8)	From acquisition and import to the outage of ATCS (T_{m8})	Parameters such as vertical visibility and horizontal visibility etc. (g_8)
9	Airport weather forecasts (l_9)	Weather conditions of the airport and nearby regions (o_9)	From the present to the next weather forecast (T_{h9})	Images and data on the distribution and intensity of wind, cloud, rain, snow, fog and thunder (f_9)	Weather information query subsystem (c_9)	From acquisition and import to the outage of ATCS (T_{m9})	Images and data on the distribution and intensity of wind, cloud, rain, snow, fog and thunder (g_9)

	(l_i)	(o_i)	(T_{hi})	(f_i)	(c_i)	(T_{mi})	(g_i)
10	(l_9) Significant weather alerts	(o_9) Regional weather condition	(T_{h9}) Sometime in the future	(f_9) Images and data on the time, intensity and distribution of severe weather conditions like wind, cloud, rain, snow, fog and thunder	(c_9) Weather information query subsystem	(T_{m9}) From acquisition and import to the outage of ATCS	(g_9) Images and data on the time, intensity and distribution of severe weather conditions like wind, cloud, rain, snow, fog and thunder
11	(l_{10}) Weather images	(o_{10}) Regional weather condition	(T_{h10}) From a certain moment in the past to the next renewal of weather forecast	(f_{10}) Images and data on the distribution and intensity of wind, cloud, rain, snow, fog and thunder	(c_{10}) Comprehensive information display subsystem	(T_{m10}) From acquisition and import to the outage of ATCS	(g_{10}) Images and data on the distribution and intensity of wind, cloud, rain, snow, fog and thunder
12	(l_{11}) Air traffic control regulations	(o_{11}) Decisions made by Government or the delegates of authoritative institutions	(T_{h11}) The time of issuing the decisions	(f_{11}) Regulation such as the sector regulations and airway transfer regulations	(c_{11}) Data maintenance subsystem	(T_{m11}) From acquisition and import to the outage of ATCS	(g_{11}) Regulation such as the sector regulations and route transfer regulations
13	(l_{12}) Agreements with surrounding areas	(o_{12}) Consensus of delegates from various departments	(T_{h12}) The time of signing agreements	(f_{12}) Agreements with neighboring restricted areas on airway use and transfer etc.	(c_{12}) Data maintenance subsystem	(T_{m12}) From acquisition and import to the outage of ATCS	(g_{12}) Agreements with neighboring restricted areas on airway use and transfer etc.
14	(l_{13}) Procedures for handling special circumstances	(o_{13}) Decisions made by department managers	(T_{h13}) The time of completing stipulations	(f_{13}) Procedures and duties for handling heavy weather, flight accidents etc.	(c_{13}) Data maintenance subsystem	(T_{m13}) From acquisition and import to the outage of ATCS	(g_{13}) Procedures and duties for handling heavy weather, flight accidents etc.

(continued)

Table 5.1 (continued)

No.	Information type	Noumenon	State occurrence time	State set	Carrier	Reflection time	Reflection set
	(l_{14})	(o_{14})	(T_{h14})	(f_{14})	(c_{14})	(T_{m14})	(g_{14})
15	Aircraft performance parameters	Various known types of plane	From the last issuance to the latest renewal	Parameters such as range, fuel load, flight altitude, flight speed etc.	Data maintenance subsystem	From acquisition and import to the outage of ATCS	Parameters such as range, fuel load, flight altitude, flight speed etc.
	(l_{15})	(o_{15})	(T_{h15})	(f_{15})	(c_{15})	(T_{m15})	(g_{15})
16	Other data codes	Relevant Objective objects and subjective cognitions	From the last import of data to the next renewal	Code dictionaries such as airport code, place name code, telegraph code, abbreviation dictionary etc.	Data maintenance subsystem	From acquisition and import to the outage of ATCS	Code dictionaries such as airport code, place name code, telegraph code, abbreviation dictionary etc.
	(l_{16})	(o_{16})	(T_{h16})	(f_{16})	(c_{16})	(T_{m16})	(g_{16})

$$o \supseteq \bigcup_{i=1}^{16} o_i, \quad T_h \supseteq \bigcup_{i=1}^{16} T_{hi}, \quad f \supseteq \bigcup_{i=1}^{16} f_i, \quad c \supseteq \bigcup_{i=1}^{16} c_i, \quad T_m \supseteq \bigcup_{i=1}^{16} T_{mi} \quad \text{and} \quad g \supseteq \bigcup_{i=1}^{16} g_i$$

denote the noumenon, state occurrence time, state set, carrier, reflection time and reflection set of information I in ATCS respectively.

$$I_i = \langle o_i, T_{hi}, f_i, c_i, T_{mi}, g_i \rangle \quad (i = 1, 2, \cdots, 16)$$

Here, the relation between the former and the latter items in the equations is "$\supseteq$" but not "$=$" because Table 5.1 only lists the typical information of ATCS but not all.

5.3 The Information Metrics for ATCS

5.3.1 ATCS Volume

In ATCS, the airspace capacity is a significant technical indicator which describes the traffic volume that ATCS is able to process. ATCS has to decide the means to process new tracks, including overload fault-tolerance processing, according to the number of tracks that have to be processed by the system at any moment. The track number is the traffic volume and it is in fact an indicator of the scope of the flight information in ATCS. Specifically, for the flight information I_1 in ATCS, the noumenon o_1 is consisted of the flights, other flying objects and the subjective consciousness of all pilots.

It is obvious that in ATCS, all kinds of information will take up some storage capacity of their carriers. For example, flight information I_1 will take up the storage capacity of radar, secondary radar and the integrated display subsystem, while airport information I_2 will take up that of the data maintenance subsystem. The demand for storage capacity, $\sigma(c_1)$ and $\sigma(c_2)$, is the volume of the corresponding information, with bit as its unit of measurement. It has to be particularly emphasized that communication system, as a special carrier of ATCS, can only function normally when it fulfills the transmission of information from one subsystem to another, i.e. from one carrier to another, in a certain time period. In this case, the information volume will impose a clear requirement on the capability of communication system.

Zhang et al. [1] conducts a simulation experiment of the transmission of flight information I_1 between airplanes and ground stations based on the VDL Model 2 communication system in the aeronautical telecommunication network. It finds out how throughput varies along with the number of airplanes and the message length (Fig. 5.1). Here the throughput is the ratio of effective information amount transmitted by communication system while the different message lengths, namely 512 Byte, 220 Byte and 96 Byte, are the volumes of one piece of flight information sent by one plane under different conditions. Figure 5.1 shows that the message lengths have clear influences over the system's throughput ratio, which means that information volume is the key element affecting the effectiveness of information

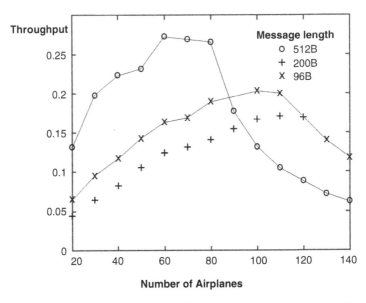

Fig. 5.1 Throughput changes with the number of airplanes and the message length [3]

Table 5.2 Occurrence probabilities of airplane state and their code formats

State symbol a_i	Occurrence probability $p(a_i)$	Code format	Code length K_i
a_1	0.20	10	2
a_2	0.19	11	2
a_3	0.18	000	3
a_4	0.17	001	3
a_5	0.15	010	3
a_6	0.10	0110	4
a_7	0.10	0111	4

transmission when the transmission ways and the communication system capabilities are certain.

We can further assume that there is a piece of state information X in the message sent from the airplane to the ground station, with a value range of $a_i(i = 1, \cdots, 7)$, representing 7 different kinds of working states respectively. Commonly, we can set a 3-bit code in the message for X to indicate its specific state. If the probabilities of occurrence for each state are the same, according to its Shannon entropy $H(X) = \sum_{i=1}^{7} \frac{1}{7} log_2 7 = log_2 7 = 2.808 bit/$symbol, the actual information volume of X is only 2.808 bits. If the probabilities of occurrence for each state are not the same, the actual information volume of X will drop further. Take Table 5.2 as an example, according to its Shannon entropy, $H(X) = -\sum_{i=1}^{7} p(a_i) log_2 p(a_i) = 2.61\ bit/$symbol, the actual information volume of X is only 2.61 bits. Its average code length is

$$\overline{K} = \sum_{i=1}^{7} p(a_i)K_i = 2.72 \ bit/symbol,$$

according to the Huffman encoding format.

It is thus clear that, according to Shannon entropy, the message length of state information X doesn't have to be 3 bits, but 2.72 bits is enough in statistical sense if Huffman encoding is adopted. When the message of flight information contains large amount of such information, we could apply Shannon entropy equation to designing the specific code format of information, so as to shorten the message length and reduce the volume of information to a large extent. Thus it is of great significance for improving communication quality.

5.3.2   ATCS Delay

As it takes time to collect, transmit and process information, there will be a certain degree of delay from state occurrence to reflection in the carrier for all kinds of information. For every piece of atomic information $I_\lambda = (o_\lambda, T_{h\lambda}, f_\lambda, c_\lambda, T_{m\lambda}, g_\lambda,)$ of the flight information $I_1 = \langle o_1, T_{h1}, f_1, b_1, T_{m1}, g_1 \rangle$ in ATCS, o_λ is a specific flying object and $T_{h\lambda}$ is its state occurrence time, then we can get that $supT_{h\lambda} = T_{h\lambda}$. As $T_{m\lambda}$ is actually the time when I_λ stays on Carrier o_λ, $infT_{m\lambda}$ is the first moment when ATCS captures I_λ. So $infT_{m\lambda} - \ sup \ T_{h\lambda}$ is the delayed time that it takes for the state information of flying object o_λ at $T_{h\lambda}$ to reach ATCS, and

$$delay(I_1) = max_{\lambda \in \Lambda}\{ \ inf \ T_{m\lambda} - supT_{h\lambda}\}$$

is the maximum delay that it takes for the state information of all flying objects to reach ATCS.

Figure 5.2 shows how the delay of the flight information sent from airplane to ground station in ATCS is influenced by the number of airplanes and the data updating rate [1]. When the number of airplanes reaches 120 and the message updates at a rate of $2s/time$, the delay exceeds 3s—the ceiling system requirement and other means of communication should be adopted in order to meet the requirement.

5.3.3   ATCS Scope

Assuming   that $o'_1 := \{a | any \ flying \ object \ processed \ by \ ATCS \ at \ time \ T_{h1}\}$ and $o'_2 := \{p | the \ subjective \ consciousness \ of \ all \ pilots \ at \ time \ T_{h1}\}$, then

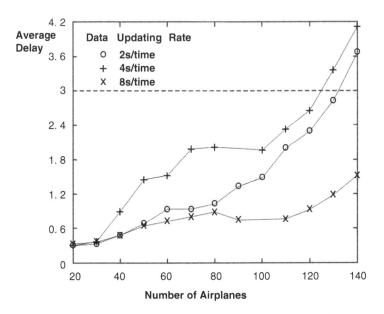

Fig. 5.2 Delay changes with the number of planes and the rate of data update [3]

$$o_1 = o'_1 \cup o'_2.$$

Here, we can define the measure of o_1, denoted by μ_1, as the number of flying objects processed by ATCS, namely $\mu_1(o_1) = |o'_1|$, where $|o'_1|$ is the potential of the set o'_1. So one of the indicators of the scope of the flight information in ATCS is

$$scope_{\mu_1}(I_1(f_1(o_1, T_{h1}))) = |o'_1|,$$

which is also the traffic volume of ATCS at time T_{h1}, whose upper limit is the airspace capacity of ATCS.

On the other hand, statistics indicate that 70% of flight accidents are caused by human factors, of which psychological factors form a major part [2]. It is generally considered that the pilot's psychology can be influenced by such factors as his/her age, flying hours, degree of education, duties during flight and whether he/she smokes, as well as the age and type of the airplane. To have a timely understanding of all pilots' consciousness status before or during the flight is critical for improving flight quality and avoiding or reducing flight accidents. So it is important for ATCS to collect the pilots' subjective consciousness as much as possible, in order to ensure flight safety. In fact, the flight current intent and the trajectory change point, etc. in ATCS are all judgments and predictions of the pilots' subjective consciousness. Now we can define another measure of o_1, denoted by μ_2, as the number of pilots whose subjective consciousness is understood by ATCS at time T_{h1}, namely

$\mu_2(o_1) = |b_2'|$, where $|o_2'|$ refers to the number of pilots in the set o_2'. Then another indicator of the scope of information I_1 in ATCS is

$$scope_{\mu_2}(I_1(f_1(o_1, T_{h1}))) = |o_2'|$$

It reflects ATCS's understanding of the subjective consciousness of all pilots of the flying objects.

The technical attribute of the airspace refers to the Information Field formed through various technical methods [2]. The airspace range, within which flight information service could be provided, is also a significant indicator of ATCS. For any flying object a in o_1', there is a perception space s_a for ATCS, namely when a is in the space s_a, it can be perceived and processed by ATCS. Thus, if we define $\bigcup_{a \in o_1'} s_a$

as the perception space of o_1' and $P_\perp\left(\bigcup_{a \in o_1'} s_a\right)$ as the orthogonal projection of $\bigcup_{a \in o_1'} s_a$

on the ground, we can get another measure of o_1, namely $\mu_3(o_1) = S\left(P_\perp\left(\bigcup_{a \in o_1'} s_a\right)\right)$

, where $S\left(P_\perp\left(\bigcup_{a \in o_1'} s_a\right)\right)$ refers to the area of $P_\perp\left(\bigcup_{a \in o_1'} s_a\right)$. Then, another indicator

of the scope of flight information I_1 is

$$scope_{\mu_3}(I_1(f_1(o_1, T_{h1}))) = S\left(P_\perp\left(\bigcup_{a \in o_1'} s_a\right)\right)$$

which reflects the airspace range within which ATCS is able to provide flight information service.

5.3.4 ATCS Granularity

The navigation chart information I_5 in ATCS is consisted of various navigation charts and different charts have different measuring scales. For example, generally speaking, the measuring scale for a worldwide navigation chart is $1 : 1000000$, that for a regional one is $1 : 500000$, and that for an airport chart is $1 : 10000$. In fact, these measuring scales reflect the different granularity of the navigation chart information.

Assuming that a certain navigation chart $I_5'\left(f_5'\left(o_5', T_{h5}'\right)\right) \subseteq I_5(f_5(o_5, T_{h5}))$, the Noumenon o_λ of its atomic information $I_\lambda(f_\lambda(o_\lambda, T_{h\lambda}))$ is the area that corresponds to a single pixel. We can define the measure of o_λ, denoted by μ_5', as its area, namely

$\mu'_5(o_\lambda) = S(o)$ $(S(o_\lambda)$ refers to the area of o_λ), and then get the granularity of information $I'_5(f'_5(o'_5, T'_{h5}))$

$$granularity_{\mu'_5}(I'_5(f'_5(o'_5, T'_{h5}))) = max_{\lambda \in \Lambda}\{S(o_\lambda)\}$$

When the measuring scales used in the navigation chart are identical, $max_{\lambda \in \Lambda}\{S(o_\lambda)\}$ is no different from any specific $S(o_\lambda)$, and its reciprocal is exactly the measuring scale of the chart. However, if the navigation chart is composed of several parts with different measuring scales, then the reciprocal of $max_{\lambda \in \Lambda}\{S(o_\lambda)\}$ is the coarsest measuring scale of the whole chart.

On the other hand, ATCS must make correlations among different radar tracks so as to exclude false targets. For primary tracks, only location and speed correlation could be conducted; for secondary and primary-secondary tracks, code correlation must be conducted before location and speed correlation. These processing demonstrate the resolving power of ATCS and in fact also reflect the detailedness of the flight information. Namely, for flight information I_1, $I_\lambda(f_\lambda(o_\lambda, T_{h\lambda}))$ which reflects the flight status of any flying object o_λ at time $T_{h\lambda}$ is the atomic information of I_1.

For o_λ, there exists a neighborhood space δ_{o_λ} which centers around o_λ at the radius of the distance resolution threshold d_λ, and we can define the measure of o_λ, denoted by $\tilde{\mu}_1$, as the volume of δ_{o_λ}, namely, $\tilde{\mu}_1(o_\lambda) = V(\delta_{o_\lambda})$ $(V(\delta_{o_\lambda})$ refers to the volume of δ_{o_λ}), then the granularity of information I_1 can be obtained

$$granularity_{\tilde{\mu}_1}(I_1(f_1(o_1, T_{h1})) = max_{\lambda \in \Lambda}\{V(\delta_{o_\lambda})\},$$

which in fact reflects the maximum distance resolution of ATCS for different flying objects. Similarly, we can define the granularity of the flight information based on the speed resolution threshold to reflect the speed resolution of ATCS. These are all significant indicators of the information processing of ATCS.

5.3.5 ATCS Variety

The specific contents of the navigation chart information in ATCS is listed in Table 5.3 and there are all together 26 items of them. That is to say, the State Set of information I_5, denoted by $f_5(o_5, T_{h5})$, contains 26 items of graphic information, namely $f_5(o_5, T_{h5}) = \{f_{5-i} | i = 1, 2, \cdots, 26\}$. Here, the potential of $f_5(o_5, T_{h5})$, denoted by $|f(o, T_h)|$, equals the number of the graphic information categories in it, and its measure is defined as

$$\rho(f(o, T_h)) = |f(o, T_h)|.$$

Then we can get the definition of the variety of $I_5(f_5(o_5, T_{h5}))$:

Table 5.3 Navigation chart information

Airport map (f_{5-1})	Regional route map (f_{5-2})	Medium low route map (f_{5-3})	International route map (f_{5-4})
Regional map (f_{5-5})	Standard instrument approach map (f_{5-6})	Standard instrument departure map (f_{5-7})	Parking plan (f_{5-8})
Instrument approach charts (f_{5-9})	Air corridor and forbidden area chart (f_{5-10})	Dumping area map (f_{5-11})	Route manual and revised data (f_{5-12})
A-shaped chart of airport obstacles (f_{5-13})	Precision approach of topographic map (f_{5-14})	Emergency back field map (f_{5-15})	Visual approach map (f_{5-16})
Visual departure map (f_{5-17})	Visual approach chart (f_{5-18})	Deployment route map (f_{5-19})	Holding flight airspace (f_{5-20})
Artificial rainfall map (f_{5-21})	Gun-launching area map (f_{5-22})	Sector chart (f_{5-23})	Temporary restricted zone chart (f_{5-24})
Temporary danger zone chart (f_{5-25})	Temporary forbidden area map (f_{5-26})		

$$\text{variety}_R(I_5)) = \left| [f(o_5, T_{h5})]_R \right|$$

which reflects the variety of the navigation chart information in ATCS.

Similarly, we can get the State Set of the information set $I(f(o, T_h))$ in ATCS from Table 5.3, i.e. $f(o, T_h) = \{f(o_i, T_{hi}) | i = 1, 2, \cdots, 16\}$. The measure of its variety, denoted by $\text{variety}_R(I) = |[f(o_i, T_{hi})]_R|$, also reflects the variety of the information in ATCS.

5.3.6   ATCS Duration

For any flying object o_λ, there is track data information $I_\lambda(f_\lambda(o_\lambda, T_{h\lambda}))$ in the flight information I_1 of ATCS that reflects its track in the airspace range of ATCS, satisfying that $I_1(f_1(o_1, T_{h1})) = \bigcup_{\lambda \in \Lambda} I_\lambda(f_\lambda(o_\lambda, T_{h\lambda}))$. A flight track is the motion trail of a flying object, which is formed by a series of discrete location reporting points. $T_{h\lambda}$ is the time set that corresponds to the discrete location reporting points of o_λ, which constitutes a finite time sequence, namely $T_{h\lambda} = \{t | t = t_1, t_2, \cdots, t_n\}$, n is the number of disperse location reporting points. The measure of $T_{h\lambda}$, denoted by τ, can be defined as the number of disperse location reporting points, denoted by n, and then we can get a definition of the duration of $I_\lambda(f_\lambda(o_\lambda, T_{h\lambda}))$

$$\text{duration}_\tau(I_\lambda(f_\lambda(o_\lambda, T_{h\lambda}))) = n.$$

Its significance lies in that, generally speaking, when the time span of $T_{h\lambda}$ is certain, namely when $t_n - t_1$ is certain, the higher the duration and the sampling rate is, the more assuring the track quality of o_λ will be; when the average sampling interval in $T_{h\lambda}$ is certain, namely when $(t_n - t_1)/(n - 1)$ is certain, the higher the duration is and the longer the maintenance time of the track is, the more assuring the control of ATCS over the track will be. At this point, a concise definition of the duration of I_1 can be given:

$$\text{duration}_\tau(I_1(f_1(b_1, T_{h1}), o_1, T_{m1})) = \sum_{\lambda \in \Lambda}\text{duration}_\tau(I_\lambda(f_\lambda(b_\lambda, T_{h\lambda}), o_\lambda, T_{m\lambda})).$$

In ATCS, for specific objects and time slots, it is possible to propose other definitions of duration under specific restraining conditions under research needs, such as the duration of the flight information during special periods like taking off and landing, so as to demonstrate the time-enriched requirements of system applications and control for different information.

5.3.7 ATCS Sampling Rate

In ATCS, the operation of the flight trajectory consists of a series of discrete location with spatiotemporal information. The report with the point of trajectory information reflects the parameters on object motion such as position, speed, heading. The parameter value are acquired with various sensors, and the process of the flight data acquisition is sampling actually. The sampling rate of ATCS reflects the sampling interval of information and is closely related to the reducibility of information. The higher the degree of detailed track information, the more timely and accurate the monitoring of flight status.

Specifically, the flight information I_1 in ATCS has a track information $I_\lambda(f_\lambda(o_\lambda, T_{h\lambda}))$ reflecting the flight object o_λ in the airspace range of ATCS. $T_{h\lambda}$ is the time set corresponding to the discrete position reporting points of o_λ, which constitutes a finite time series. That is, $T_{h\lambda} = \{t | t = t_1, t_2, \cdots, t_n\}$, n is the number of reporting points in discrete positions. For any $\lambda \in \Lambda$, there are $U_\lambda \subseteq [\inf T_h, \quad \sup T_h]$, $T_h \cap U_\lambda = \varnothing$, where Λ is an index set of ATCS track data. Then, the sampling rate of I_λ is the ratio of the cardinality of Λ to the Lebesgue measure $|U|$ of $U = \bigcup_{\lambda \in \Lambda} U_\lambda$.

$$\text{sampling\_rate}(I) = \frac{|\Lambda|}{|U|}.$$

5.3.8   ATCS Aggregation

In ATCS, flight track is important data. The aggregation degree of ATCS reflects the correlation degree of flight information content. By measuring the similarity between different voyage information, the same voyage information is gathered, different voyage information is separated, and the voyage trajectory is divided into different clusters. With the clustering algorithm, the trajectory of flight history is grouped, and the normal flight trajectory model of aircraft is constructed. It may lay the foundation for real-time detection of abnormal flight trajectory, and then provide a new method to improve the intelligent level of air traffic supervision.

Specifically, for ATCS, let $\mathcal{F}$ be the set of all flight trajectory of flight o on time T_h, and $(\mathcal{F}, 2^{\mathcal{F}}, l)$ be the flight trajectory measure space, l is the navigation trajectory model measure on the navigation trajectory measurable set $2^{\mathcal{F}}$, The navigation trajectory information $I = (o, T_h, f, c, T_m, g)$, and the clustering degree of navigation trajectory model measure l $clustering_l(I)$ is the navigation trajectory model measure $l(f(o, T_h))$ of $f(o, T_h)$ on the measurable set $2^{\mathcal{F}}$, i.e

$$clustering_l(I) = l(f(o, T_h))$$

where, the $l(f(o, T_h)) = \dfrac{\sum_{i,j \in clu} d(f(o_i, T_h), f(o_j, T_h))}{\sum_{i,j \notin clu} d(f(o_i, T_h), f(o_j, T_h))}$, clu is a cluster, d for similarity measure.

5.3.9   ATCS Coverage

The value of a network system is equal to the product of the maximum scope and the maximum coverage of all contained information. In ATCS, information such as airport real weather I_7, airport weather forecast I_9 and significant weather alert I_{10} is all carried by the subsystem of meteorological information query. The subsystem is further comprised of World Area Forecast System (WAFS), central database cluster and numerous clients, which are all carriers of meteorological information. Assuming that ATCS consists of WAFS, central database cluster and 498 clients, and the updated region distribution of lightning I_0 has got reflected in WAFS, central database cluster and 448 clients but not in the rest 50 clients, then the coverage of this information in ATCS is

$$coverage_{I_0}(I) = \frac{450}{500}$$

The 50 clients that haven't got the updated *regional distribution of lightning* are obviously restricted in terms of their ability to dispatch and control flights although they still have the old information. Therefore, the coverage of information exerts important influence on the overall running of ATCS.

5.3.10 ATCS Distortion

In ATCS, flight information I_1 reflects such parameters of the flying object as location, speed and course, which might bear some differences from the real status due to errors in the measurement, transmission and processing sessions. We use $f_1(o_1, T_{h1})$ to denote the real motion state of the airplane. According to $g_1(c_1, T_{m1})$, no matter it is graph or data, we could infer the motion state of the flying object, denoted by $\widetilde{f}_1\left(\widetilde{o}_1', \widetilde{T}_{h1}'\right)$, based on common sense. The difference between $f_1(o_1, T_{h1})$ and $\widetilde{f}_1\left(\widetilde{o}_1', \widetilde{T}_{h1}'\right)$ reflects the system error of ATCS, which is the validity of I_1. Figure 5.3 displays the error correction results of flight information before and after fusion of data from ADS and 3 SSR systems in ATCS, from which we can see that different Carriers of flight information differ greatly from each other and that data fusion could reduce errors and improve the validity of information. The root-mean-square error after data fusion as listed in Table 5.4 is the validity of flight information.

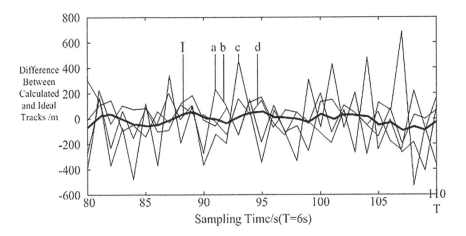

Fig. 5.3 Simulation results of ADS-SSR fusion [3]

Table 5.4 Root-mean-square errors of ATCS sensors and systems

	ADS	SSR1	SSR2	SSR3	After fusion
Root-mean-square (m)	58.72	65.77	37.94	30.25	23.85

5.3.11 *ATCS Mismatch*

Different users have different demands for information and the suitability of information also differs from person to person. Take the information in ATCS as an example, for a governor of the overall situation and a specific user focusing only on one specific flight, the connotation and measure of information suitability will be hugely different.

For governors of the overall situation, all the items of information and their component elements listed in Table 5.1 are essential to the information set of ATCS. There is a specific target set for the elements of each information item and the distance spaces $\langle (\mathcal{P}_o, \mathcal{P}_{T_h}, \mathcal{P}_f, \mathcal{P}_c, \mathcal{P}_{T_m}, \mathcal{P}_g), d \rangle$ should ascertain the distance through the coverage of target set. Thus the suitability of the information in ATCS, is able to support the design, exploration and assessment of ATCS.

For specific users who focus only on specific flights, we can get the information suitability for individual users with the specific flight, flying time, flying status, information system, display time and display mode as focus, and with the degree of matchability between information elements and the focus as measure. Future ATCS should be able to not only provide comprehensive information support to governors of the overall situation but also offer personalized information service to single users.

Therefore, for all eleven metrics of information, we could find a series of actual indexes in ATCS that correspond to them, such as airspace capacity, target resolution ratio, data sampling rate, message length, system delay and data precision, most of which reflect the key capabilities of ATCS. Out of the need for concise exposition, usually we only choose certain proper sub-information $I' \subseteq I = \langle o, T_h, f, c, T_m, g \rangle$ in ATCS for analysis instead of analyzing I directly. However, this does not affect the rationality of the exposition, since the measure of its sub-information I' can also be considered a measure of I itself.

5.4 Chapter Summary

ATCS is a comprehensive system that integrates control staff, control automation equipment, control operation environment, and various operation management mechanisms and rules. It aims to ensure the safe flight of aircraft and accelerate and maintain an orderly air traffic flow. This chapter analyzes the objective information in ATCS, establishes an objective information model, and analyzes the information measurement model of ATCS based on the measurement system of objective information theory, which can assist system construction and control departments to clearly grasp the operating status and trend of ATCS, and facilitate their implementation of control In the process, the operation of the control system is coordinated and managed to help the control department equationte long-term and effective control measures and control system operation plans, thereby increasing the control capacity, ensuring the safety and normality of flights, and accelerating the flow of air traffic.

References

1. Zhang, J., et al.: Modern Air Traffic Management (in Chinese). Beijing University of Aeronautics and Astronautics Press, Beijing (2005)
2. Li, G., Baker, S.P., Grabowski, J.G., Rebok, G.W.: Human factors in aviation crashes involving older pilots. Aviat. Space Environ. Med. **73**(2), 134–138 (2002)
3. Xu, J., Wang, S., Liu, Z., Wang, Y.: Objective information theory exemplified in air traffic control system. Chin. J. Electron. **30**(4), 743–751 (2021)

Chapter 6
Exemplifying Objective Information Theory: Smart Court

Abstract It is a worldwide engineering challenge to develop large-scale complex information systems such as Smart Court. The nationwide construction, application and promotion of the Smart Court system-of-systems engineering project of China guarantee the upgrade and reshaping of the judicial operation pattern of Chinese people's courts. It has gained remarkable achievements and brought China to the leading position in judicial informatization in the world. In this chapter, OIT is applied to explain the behavior of Smart Court for demonstrating the feasibility and practicality to investigate system-of-systems.

Keywords Objective information theory (OIT) · Smart Courts in China · Smart Court SoSs engineering project · Exemplification

6.1 Smart Court

Smart Court is a form of organization, construction, operation and management of people's courts based on modern information technology that realizes online transaction of all businesses, publishing of all the procedures according laws as well as providing comprehensive smart service. It is centered on the provision of justice for the people and judicial impartiality and adheres to the integration of judicial rules, institutional reform and technology innovation [1]. The operation of the Smart Court system is a typical complex giant system problem [2]. The factors affecting the operation results include basic equipment factors, user behavior factors, etc., and there are many cross-influences between them, so it is difficult to simply adopt a hierarchical index system [3]. According to the top-level design of the complex system, each system-level component is an information system that manages objective information.

6.1.1 Component Systems

The construction of Smart Courts in China involves more than 3000 regular courts, 10,000 dispatched courts, and 4000 collaborative departments nationwide. The number of information systems, such as infrastructure systems, intelligent applications, data management, network security, and operation and maintenance support, has exceeded 13,000. These systems operate relatively independently and simultaneously every day at a large scale and with a wide spatial distribution and varying durations. It is an extremely complicated SoSs engineering project, featuring heterogeneous systems, various functions and tasks, numerous collaborative departments, and close sharing and linkage.

Figure 6.1 is the reference model of the Smart Court SoSs, which presents the main components and their relations as a whole. As shown in Fig. 6.1, the core of the Smart Court SoSs of information systems is the Judicial Big Data Management and Service Platform, which gathers various types of operation data of the Smart Court and knowledge resources generated from the data. The intelligent service, intelligent trial, intelligent execution, and intelligent management systems at the inner ring are

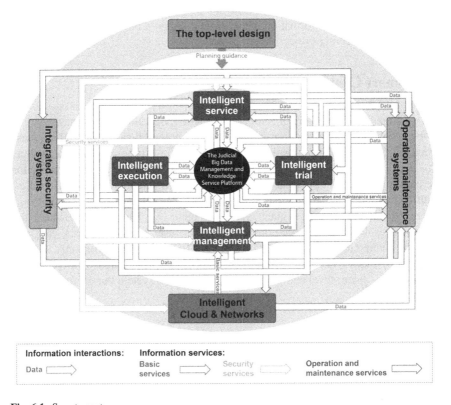

Fig. 6.1 Smart court

Table 6.1 The typical systems in the Smart Court SoSs

Type	Typical systems
Intelligent service	People's Court Online Service (Former name: China Mobile Micro-Court)
	People's Court Mediation Platform
	Litigation Service Network
	12368 Litigation Service Hotline
	Electronic Service Platform
	Online Preservation Platform
	Online Identification Platform
	etc.
Intelligent trial	Trial Process Management Platform
	Electronic File Transfer Application
	Intelligent Trial Assistance System
	etc.
Intelligent execution	Executive Command Management Platform
	Information Management System of Execution Case Process
	Network Execution Check and Control System
	Joint Credit Disciplinary System
	Online Judicial Auction Platform
	Inquiry Evaluation System
	"One Account A Case" Management Platform
	Mobile execution System·etc.
Intelligent management	Online Office Platform
	Trial Supervision Platform
	Electronic Archives System

the main carriers for the Smart Courts to serve different users, some typical systems are shown in Table 6.1. The Intelligent Cloud & Networks, integrated security systems, and operation maintenance systems at the outer ring are the basis and guarantee conditions for the operation of the Smart Courts. In addition, the top-level design is referred to as a collection of tasks such as planning, design, and always been emphasized in the construction of the Smart Court SoSs engineering project.

Not only does this reference model, featuring one-core and two-rings, take into account the characteristics of general information system, but also aims at the main operations of the Smart Court. Notably, the emphasis that designers should not only consider the main components of the SoSs but also their interactions is where this reference model mostly differs from other technical reference models. This consideration is also the key requirement that has always been emphasized in the construction of the Smart Court SoSE project. Here, the interactions are actually the information relations, on which the SoSs design methods are based. Wherein, the information relations between these four types of application systems, that is, the intelligent service, intelligent trial, intelligent execution, and intelligent management, is mainly information interaction. In the meantime, the application systems all have interactions with the Judicial Big Data Management and Knowledge Service

Platform, and are supported by information services of the Intelligent Cloud & Networks, integrated security systems, and operation maintenance systems.

The Judicial Big Data Management and Service Platform provides data and knowledge services for the four types of application systems. The Intelligent Cloud & Networks is referred to as the sum of various types of information infrastructures, which provides basic services such as computing, storage, database, and communication networks for various application systems, the Judicial Big Data Management and Service Platform, integrated security systems, and operation maintenance systems. The integrated security systems are the set of systems that provide various security protections such as identity authentication, border protection, security supervision, and so on, as well as information security services for other systems. The operation maintenance systems are a set of information systems for the insurance of system operation, treatment of system faults, and evaluation of operation quality and effectiveness, thereby providing operation and maintenance services for other systems.

6.1.2   Integrating Systems

In the construction of Smart Court SoSs, besides the research, development and promotion of typical information systems, it is also a central task to integrate various systems and continuously improve the collaboration between systems, the integration of a collaborative framework includes the following main components:

- Basic integration: connect and integrate the information infrastructure distributed countrywide, including the private court network that connects tier-four courts and all the dispatched tribunals nationwide, to realize interconnections among the Internet, external private network, mobile private network, and confidential network on the premise of complying with the security isolation standards. Meanwhile, with the further popularization of cloud computing facilities and their deep integration with the communication network, the intelligent voice cloud platform of national courts is being constructed, utilizing cloud resources and cloud services as an integrated infrastructure to provide unified communications, computing, storage, and intelligent support capabilities.
- Data integration: build up the Judicial Big Data Management and Service Platform of the People's Court and the data center for higher courts and above, realize the physical or logical aggregation of data resources distributed in local courts and all types of application systems, and conduct quality inspection, correction, and association based on the corresponding data quality criteria. In addition, continue improving and consolidating the volume, delay, scope, granularity, variety, duration, sampling rate, aggregation, convergence, distortion, and mismatch of judicial big data, and build an integrated data space to fully support the data exchange and sharing of all types of information systems.

- Knowledge integration: based on the rich resources of judicial big data, comprehensively utilize multimodal artificial intelligence technologies, such as text, voice, video, and natural language processing, through large-scale manual tagging, automated deep learning, and the confluence of professional knowledge; a unified judicial knowledge base and a judicial knowledge service engine are established based on legal rules and historical cases, which are suitable for different application scenarios, fully support the full dimensional, integrated, and large-scale application of judicial artificial intelligence, and significantly improve the intelligent auxiliary ability of information systems.
- Application integration: promote intelligent services, trials, executions, and management systems, mainly through online services, trial case processing, execution case processing, and office automation, respectively. With the Judicial Big Data Management and Service Platform as the core and a series of auxiliary intelligent applications as the entrance, a highly integrated application system-of-systems, which fully supports information exchange, data sharing, and operation linkage of all types of business applications, is formed.
- Service integration: in view of the trend of reducing costs and increasing efficiency, as well as the increasing popularity of cloud service technologies and systems, such as IaaS, PaaS, and SaaS, it is necessary to promote more information system resources to support Smart Court applications in a service-oriented fashion. Consequently, a physically distributed and centralized management service resource system has been initially built up. It can efficiently support unified collection, unified evaluation, unified release, and selective services of various information services.
- Portal integration: for specific users on the court private network, Internet or confidential network, integrated, personalized, and customized unified entrance portals are provided according to the characteristics of PC, mobile, and different operating systems, respectively. Consequently, all types of users can benefit from being familiar with the access, operation, and obtaining of abundant information in the Smart Court information system.

The above integration in Smart Court can realize many collaborative capabilities, such as system interconnection, information exchange, data sharing, intelligent assistance, and operation linkage, which is impossible in a single or local system. It also can explore many collaborative services and support capabilities beyond the designer's prior knowledge. For example, the integration of multiple previously unrelated systems may produce brand-new system functions; a variety of data associations may present inherent laws that have never been realized before, leading to a new service model. These phenomena, called "emergence", are not only an important feature of SoSE but also the key content of the integration of collaborative systems of the Smart Court, which deserve further investigation.

6.2 The Sextuple of Smart Court

The information resources of Smart Court include six categories: trial execution, judicial administration, judicial personnel, judicial research, information management, and external data. We selected 13 representative typical information and analyzed the six element of each information according to OIT, as shown in Table 6.2. Among them, case filing information, hearing announcement information, audio and video information of court hearing belong to trial execution, administrative document information and news information belong to judicial affairs, personnel information and people's mediation institution information belong to judicial personnel, laws and regulations information and judicial statistics information belong to judicial research, informative assets information and information system operation information belong to information management, and lawyer information and postal service information belong to external data.

The sextuple model of OIT in Smart Court indicates the specific components of an information item.

$$I = \langle o, T_h, f, c, T_m, g \rangle.$$

where, o, T_h, f, c, T_m, g denote the noumenon, state occurrence time, state set, carrier, reflection time and reflection set of information I in Smart Court respectively. Table 6.2 depicts the typical information elements of Smart Court. 6 class, 13 typical issues, wherein $o \supseteq \bigcup_{i=1}^{13} o_i$, $T_h \supseteq \bigcup_{i=1}^{13} T_{hi}$, $f \supseteq \bigcup_{i=1}^{13} f_i$, $c \supseteq \bigcup_{i=1}^{13} c_i$, $T_m \supseteq \bigcup_{i=1}^{13} T_{mi}$ and $g \supseteq \bigcup_{i=1}^{13} g_i$ denote the noumenon, state occurrence time, state set, carrier, reflection time and reflection set of information I in Smart Court respectively.

$$I_i = \langle o_i, T_{hi}, f_i, c_i, T_{mi}, g_i \rangle \quad (i = 1, 2, \cdots, 13)$$

Here, the relation between the former and the latter items in the equations is "$\supseteq$" but not "$=$" because Table 6.2 only lists the typical information of Smart Court but not all.

6.3 The Information Metrics for Smart Court

The overall effect of the construction and application of China's Smart Court SoS depends on various efficacies produced by the integration of all the information systems as a whole. Although almost every system and every type of information movement will have an effect and impact (in part) on users' feelings and effects, the critical performance metrics of key systems will have a more important impact on the 11 metric effects of the whole system. In practice, we have formed a performance

Table 6.2 The main elements of the typical information set in Smart Court

No.	Information type	Noumenon	State occurrence time	State set	Carrier	Reflection time	Reflection set
	(I)	(o)	(T_h)	(f)	(c)	(T_m)	(g)
1	Case filing information (I_1)	Subjective consciousness of litigation parties and case filing judges (o_1)	From the beginning of filing to the end (T_{h1})	Relevant personnel's understanding and appeal of the case (f_1)	Case Handling Platform, Litigation Service Network, People's Court Online Service, etc (c_1)	From data entry into the Case Handling Platform, Litigation Service Network, People's Court Online Service and other systems to the outage of these systems (T_{m1})	Case cause, case number, filing time, litigants, main case description and other data (g_1)
2	Hearing announcement information (I_2)	The subjective consciousness of the judge (o_2)	From announcement to next update (T_{h2})	Arrangements and illustrations on the time, place, litigants and cause of action of the hearing (f_2)	Hearing announcement release system (c_2)	From data entry to the outage of the Hearing Announcement Release System (T_{m2})	Hearing time, place, litigants, cause of action and other data (g_2)
3	Audio and video information of court hearing (I_3)	The court scene environment, the subjective consciousness of litigants and judges in the trial (o_3)	From the beginning of the trial to the end (T_{h3})	The environmental status of the court scene, the language, behavior, expression, etc. of litigants and judges during the trial (f_3)	Video recorder, video camera, Science and Technology Court System (c_3)	From the beginning of the trial to the outage of the audio and video recording, storage, live broadcast, recording and broadcasting systems of the trial (T_{m3})	Hearing audio, video, image and other data (g_3)
4		The subjective consciousness of the	From the drafting of		Office platform		Text description of official documents,

(continued)

Table 6.2 (continued)

No.	Information type	Noumenon	State occurrence time	State set	Carrier	Reflection time	Reflection set
	Administrative document information	drafters of administrative documents	administrative documents to the submission	Specific contents of relevant administrative documents		From data entry to the outage of the office platform	pictures, audio and video and other supporting data
	(l_4)	(o_4)	(T_{h4})	(f_4)	(c_4)	(T_{m4})	(g_4)
5	News information	Environmental status of major activities and subjective consciousness of participants	From the beginning to the end of major activities	Specific environment, process and participant behavior of major activities	Court official website, microblog, WeChat official account, etc	From data entry to the outage of the court official website, microblog, WeChat official account, etc	Text reports, pictures, audio and video data of major activities
	(l_5)	(o_5)	(T_{h5})	(f_5)	(c_5)	(T_{m5})	(g_5)
6	Personnel information	All court officers	From the birth of a court officer to not working in the court	Resume, main work performance and subjective understanding of court officers	People's Court Personnel Management System	From data entry to the outage of the People's Court Personnel Management System	Name, work department, job title, job position, personal report, organization evaluation and other data
	(l_6)	(o_6)	(T_{h6})	(f_6)	(c_6)	(T_{m6})	(g_6)
7	People's mediation institution Information	People's mediation institutions	From the establishment to the termination of the people's mediation institutions	Name, location and jurisdiction of people's mediation institutions	People's Court Mediation Platform	From data entry to the outage of the People's Court Mediation Platform	Name, location, jurisdiction and other data of the people's mediation institution
	(l_7)	(o_7)	(T_{h7})	(f_7)	(c_7)	(T_{m7})	(g_7)
8			From the beginning of	Specific contents of laws and regulations	Laws and regulations database	From data entry to the outage of the	Laws and regulations, provisions,

No.	Information (I)	Observer (o)	T_h	f	Carrier (c)	T_m	g
	Laws and regulations information (I_8)	Subjective consciousness of legislators (o_8)	legislation to the official release of laws and regulations (T_{h8})			laws and regulations database (T_{m8})	requirements and other data (g_8)
9	Judicial statistics information (I_9)	People's courts at all levels under the jurisdiction (o_9)	From the beginning to the end of a judicial statistics (T_{h9})	Specific information on cases handled by each court (f_8)	People's Court Big Data Management and Service Platform (c_8)	From data entry to the outage of the People's Court Big Data Management and Service Platform (T_{m9})	Statistical data, tables and curves of all kinds of cases filed, closed and unsettled in the courts under their jurisdiction (g_9)
10	Informative asset information (I_{10})	Informative assets of the court in the jurisdiction (o_{10})	From asset receipt to next update (T_{h10})	Specific situation of informative assets (f_9)	Informative Asset Management System (c_9)	From data entry to the outage of the Informative Asset Management System (T_{m10})	Data and forms such as asset name, purchase time, warehousing time, storage location and management personnel (g_{10})
11	Information system operation information (I_{11})	Various information systems of the court in the jurisdiction (o_{11})	From the time when the system is online to the outage of the system (T_{h11})	Operation of information system (f_{10})	People's Court Quality and Efficiency Operation and Paintenance Management Platform (c_{10})	From the beginning of data entry to the outage of the People's Court Quality and Efficiency Operation and Paintenance Management Platform (T_{m10})	Data and charts such as the number of failures, response time and number of users of various information systems (g_{10})

(continued)

Table 6.2 (continued)

No.	Information type	Noumenon	State occurrence time	State set	Carrier	Reflection time	Reflection set
12	Lawyer information	Legal practitioner	From obtaining the lawyer's qualification certificate to outage	Specific information about lawyers	People's Court Lawyer Service Platform	From data entry to the outage of the People's Court Lawyer Service Platform	Data and forms such as lawyer's name, license type, number, practice institution, etc. have been entered
	(l_{11})	(o_{11})	(T_{h11})	(f_{11})	(c_{11})	(T_{m11})	(g_{11})
	(l_{12})	(o_{12})	(T_{h12})	(f_{12})	(c_{12})	(T_{m12})	(g_{12})
13	Postal service information	Various service documents	From the beginning to the end of service	The specific process of document delivery	Unified Service Platform of the People's Court	From data entry to the outage of the Unified Service Platform of the People's Court	Document name, delivery time, signing method and other data
	(l_{13})	(o_{13})	(T_{h13})	(f_{13})	(c_{13})	(T_{m13})	(g_{13})

indicator system of China's Smart Court SoS. There are 65 indicators in the system corresponding to the 11 metric effects. Through monitoring the changes of these indicators, we can continuously improve the operating quality and effect of the whole Smart Court.

6.3.1   Performance Indicator

The performance indicator system of China Smart Court in presented in Table 6.3. As a general SoSs can include a large number of systems, and each system may include many subsystems as well, the evaluation indicators in the table can serve as not only the comprehensive indicators but also the specific indicators for some important subsystems. Therefore, these key indicators provide an important design and evaluation basis for the implementation of the Smart Court SoSs engineering project.

6.3.2   Metric Illustrations

The changing curves of the key performance indicators of China's Smart Court SoSs in recent years are illustrated in Fig. 6.2.

- In Fig. 6.2a, the total amount of data resources on the judicial big data platform reflects the volume efficacy of the Supreme Court to gather judicial big data from courts nationwide, and its steady rise shows that the accumulation of judicial big data resources is becoming more and more abundant.
- In Fig. 6.2b, the average response latency indicator of the court office platform has dropped to less than 0.8 s since November 2020, which is related to the delay efficacy and directly affect the experience of almost all users and has won the unanimous praise of users.
- In Fig. 6.2c, since November 2021, the court video network has been steadily connected to more than 93% of the S&T courts across China in real time, which reflects the scope efficacy of the courtroom video information nationwide.
- In Fig. 6.2d, since August 2015, the case coverage rate has basically reached and remained stable at 100% nationwide, which is related to the granularity efficacy of judicial information management and fully indicates that the judicial information management has reached a very fine level (single case) nationwide.
- In Fig. 6.2e, since December 2013, when the judicial data platform was officially launched, the types of information have steadily increased, basically realizing the convergence, management and application of all information types, which is related to the variety efficacy of information gathered by the judicial big data platform, reflecting the integrity of information management.

Table 6.3 The performance indicators of Smart Court

Metric effects	Information collection	Information action	Information transmission	Information processing	Data space
Volume	• Application system input data volume	• Application system output data volume	• Communication network bandwidth	• Information Infrastructure Storage Resources • Information Infrastructure Storage Resource Utilization	• Data resources aggregated by information system
Delay	• Application system upload data delay	• Application system operation response delay	• Communication network information transmission delay	• Information infrastructure computing resources and processing rate • Information infrastructure computing resource utilization • Application system information processing delay • Security system safety protection processing delay	• Various data aggregation delay of information system
Scope	• Regional coverage and number of users of the application system	• The scope of information provided to users by the application system		• The scope of application system processing information	• Source region and department scope of all data aggregated by information system
Granularity	• Integrity rate of information items collected by application system • Resolution of video information collected by application system	• Integrity rate of information items provided by the application system to users • Resolution of output video information of application system		• Integrity rate of information items processed by application system • Resolution of video information processed by application system	• Integrity degree of information items aggregated by information system

Variety	• Number of types and methods of application system input information	• Number of types and methods of application system output information	• Number of types of information transmitted over communication network	• Number of types of information processed by application system	• Number of types of information aggregated by information systems
Duration	• Effective working time of application system • Mean time between failures of application system	• Effective working time of application system • Mean time between failures of application system	• Effective working time of communication network system • Mean time between failures of communication network system	• Effective working time of information processing system • Mean time between failures of information processing system	• Length of time of all types of information aggregated by information system
Sampling-rate	• Application system input data sampling rate	• Application system output data sampling rate	• Communication network bandwidth • Communication network bandwidth utilization	• Computing storage facility throughput • Application system information processing cycle	• Sampling periods of all types of data aggregated by information system
Aggregation		• Application system output data aggregation		• Data aggregation processed by information processing systems	• Aggregation degree of the total data aggregated by information system
Coverage		• Distribution and the number of application system users	• Communication network coverage area network	• Security system information encryption effectiveness • Accuracy of user authority control of security systems • Safety isolation reliability of inter-network security systems	• Regional distribution of information system
Distortion	• Input information accuracy of application system	• Output information accuracy of application system	• Bit error rate and packet loss rate of information transmitted over communication network	• Processing error of information processing system	• The confidence of the full data of information system

(continued)

Table 6.3 (continued)

Metric effects	Information collection	Information action	Information transmission	Information processing	Data space
Mismatch	• Application system input information mismatch	• Output information adaptability and user satisfaction of application system	• Format and type adaptability of information transmitted over communication network	• Matching accuracy of "user requirements—output data" of information processing system	• Matching accuracy of "user requirements—output data" of full data of information system

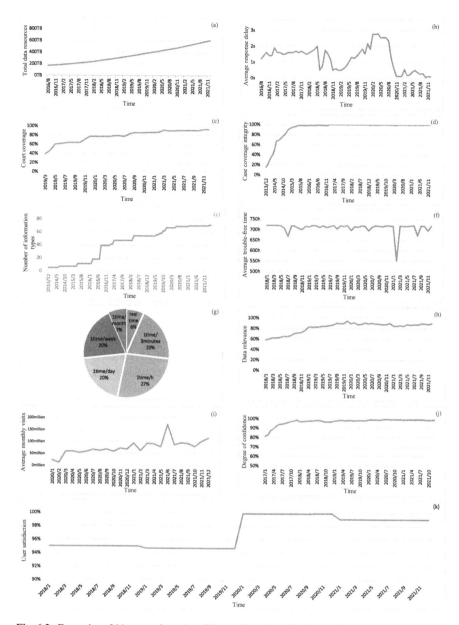

Fig. 6.2 Examples of 11 types of metrics of Smart Court SoSs [1, 3]. (**a**) Change curve of total data resources of the judicial big data platform; (**b**) Change curve of average response delay of court office platform; (**c**) Change curve of court coverage monitored to S&T Court; (**d**) Change curve of nationwide court case coverage integrity; (**e**) Change curve of information types of the judicial big data platform; (**f**) Change curve of the average trouble-free time of the information systems; (**g**) Distribution of data sampling rate of the LawEye platform; (**h**) Change curve of data relevance of the judicial big data platform; (**i**) Change curve of average monthly visits of People's Court Online Service; (**j**) Change curve of judicial statistics confidence of judicial big data platform; (**k**) Change curve of user satisfaction of information system

- In Fig. 6.2f, since March 2018, the average time between failures of the court information systems has basically remained stable at over 700 h, which is related to the duration efficacy of the court information systems. Individual periods of the significant decline will cause the inevitable shortening of the length of real-time information collection in the corresponding period.
- In Fig. 6.2g, the sampling rate of 53% of monitoring information is higher than 1 time/h and 73% of monitoring information is higher than 1 time/day on the LawEye platform. The LawEye platform monitors and manages the operating quality of court information systems nationwide, and its sampling intensity is related to the sampling-rate efficacy of the court information systems.
- In Fig. 6.2h, since January 2019, the information aggregation degree of the judicial big data platform has been higher than 80%, which is related to the aggregation efficacy of judicial big data and indicates that the association and application of information is at a good level.
- In Fig. 6.2i, since February 2020, the number of monthly visits to People's Court Online Service, a unified window serving the public, has steadily increased and exceeded 100 million by December 2021. The number of information system visits is related with the coverage efficacy of information systems, fully demonstrating the remarkable effectiveness in facilitating the public.
- In Fig. 6.2j, since January 2018, the confidence level of statistics on the judicial big data has been higher than 97% and is currently stable at more than 99% for a long period of time. The data confidence level is negative related to the distortion efficacy of information, i.e., the corresponding distortion level is lower than 1%, thus laying a credible foundation for various big data analyses and services.
- In Fig. 6.2k, since January 2020, the user satisfaction of the court information systems has been higher than 98%, which is the negative indicator of the mismatch efficacy of the court information systems, fully demonstrating the remarkable achievements of China Smart Court engineering project.

The excellent performance of China Smart Court is demonstrated by the indicators in Fig. 6.2. Specifically, all the 65 indicators in Table 6.3 are kept monitoring 24 h annually by the LawEye platform. It reflects the operation status of the critical information systems, including the aforementioned intelligent service, intelligent trial, intelligent execution, intelligent management, judicial openness, and etc. Any unusual changes of these indicators are analyzed and adjustment is conducted according to the dynamic configuration of information systems. For instance, the decrease of the amount of data resources means that the volume efficacy of the judicial big data platform is reduced. According to the dynamic configuration of China's Smart Court SoSs, the volume efficacy involves all the links of information collection, transmission, processing, action and data space. Therefore, the corresponding approaches, such as the enlargement of the storage of data space, the increase of the bandwidth of court private networks, and the data compression processing, are conducted accordingly. In fact, it is the systematically helps us to keep improving the operation quality and efficiency of China Smart Court.

Table 6.4 Changes of the indicators of building up the Smart Court 2017–2021

Court	2017	2018	2019	2020	2021
Nationwide	72	78	85	88	84.0
Supreme court	80	83	86	90	83.3
Intermediate court	70	78	86	90	84.9
Basic court	67	73	83	86	82.7

The Supreme People's Court has been conducting comprehensive evaluation through the indicators of building up the national Smart Court since 2017. Table 6.4 reflects the changes in the indicators.

In Table 6.4, the indicators of building up the Smart Court at all levels have been increasing yearly since 2017, reaching an excellent level by 2020. 2021 was the beginning of the new five-year plan, and the evaluation criteria were raised. Although the grades in 2021 decreased compared to those in the previous year, they maintained a general level higher than 80, while the actual quality and efficiency were significantly improved.

6.4 Supports from China Smart Court

The major difficulty of information engineering are "making use of it" rather than "building it up". No information system is perfect, not to mention information systems that cover all sectors vertically and main business areas—unsatisfactory aspects seem unavoidable. In the case of China Smart Court, it is precisely by relying on the strong popularization and promotion, as well as persisting in the mutual running-in and mutual promotion of "building up" and "making use" that many information applications have successfully covered the courts at all levels throughout the country to benefit the mass crowd. Meanwhile, the judicial operation pattern of Chinese courts has been reshaped in all aspects.

The Smart Court supports universal intelligent services in all time and space. In the past, mediation, filing of cases, exchange of evidence, marking, opening of hearings, consultation on litigation matters, understanding of the litigation process, attendance on court hearings, access to judicial documents, and other activities that used to be completed by parties or litigation agents in person can now be realized through the Internet. Meanwhile, the judges can utilize a dedicated network of the court to directly contact the people through the Internet based on security isolation exchanges, such that the people involved in judicial proceedings need to be present in person at most once or not even once, which significantly reduces their effort and cost in commuting.

The Smart Court supports the full process of intelligent trials assisted by intelligent technologies. The courts at all levels can instantly transmit the litigation documents presented by the parties to the trial information system, by scanning the paper-based documents submitted offline or directly uploading the electronic documents submitted online, and thus the case judges can easily review the documents and form collegium online. Meanwhile, based on the intelligent recognition and processing of file information, the trial case handling system can almost provide judges with intelligent assistance throughout the whole process, including automatic cataloging of electronic files, intelligent recommendation of legal provisions, intelligent recommendation of similar cases, auxiliary generation of legal documents, and intelligent error correction of judicial documents, etc. In addition, it can be combined with speech recognition technology to support intelligent speech recognition of the trial and automatically generate high-accuracy curt transcripts, which significantly reduces the routine work of judges and clerks.

The Smart Court supports the intelligent execution of inter-departmental coordination. Because the whole nation should be well-coordinated in the enforcement phase, the Smart Court utilizes the Internet technology to vertically connect the enforcement departments of courts at all levels across the country to realize linkages between the upper and lower levels; in the meantime, it enables the horizontal sharing of information with finance, transportation, economy, and other industries to achieve business coordination, such that the executive judges can conduct their work online without leaving the house, which was previously only possible in person, including handling of cases, process node management, executive investigation, control and punishment for breach of credibility, judicial auction, information disclosure, and executive command. The Smart Court not only reduces the time and cost spent on commuting for a large number of personnel but also provides an effective way that is difficult to achieve through traditional offline methods. Therefore, it has become a new solution for Chinese courts to solve enforcement problems effectively.

The Smart Court supports intelligent management based on judicial big data and gathers a large amount of business and technical data in real time. It has continuously accumulated six types of interrelated judicial big data resources, including trial execution, judicial personnel, judicial administration, judicial research, informatization, and external data. On this basis, online office, judicial supervision, and one-click filing can bring considerable convenience to judicial administration. The judicial statistics, personnel information management, trial situation analysis, and economic and social development research based on judicial big data have created a new approach that could not be achieved traditionally, in terms of both efficiency and accuracy.

The final effect of the Smart Court SoSE is reflected in its great contribution to the progress of judicial civilization: it enables the mass crowd to accomplish their litigation processes with the need of being in person at most one time and can reduce the clerical work of judges by more than 30%. The efficiency of the trial has been improved by more than 20%, and the solemn promise of "basically solving the difficulties in enforcement in 2–3 years" has been realized. Judicial openness has comprehensively enhanced the judicial transparency of China. The "Quality of Judicial Process Index", which mainly reflects the judicial informatization, was ranked number one in the world by the World Bank in 2020. From 2019 to 2021, it reduced public travel costs equivalent to 200,000 man-years, and saved 302.4 billion CNY in social expenses. The Smart Court in China has not only provided strong information support for social fairness and justice but also won wide attention and high praise globally. On this basis, the Supreme People's Court of China has successively issued "Online Litigation Rules of People's Courts", "Online Mediation Rules of People's Courts", and "Online Operation Rules of People's Courts", such that the joint force of advanced technology and judicial operation can be further refined in the form of judicial interpretation and normative documents. Therefore, the use of the online judicial model is effectively promoted towards a higher level of digital justice.

Due to the growing user demands and the rapid evolution of information technologies, there is still plenty of room for improvement regarding intelligence, integration, collaboration, universality, and convenience. First, there is an urgent need to constantly deepen and summarize the relevant academic theories and technical models equationted on the methodology to construct a rich and systematic SoSE model and tool system as references for the penetration of information and intelligence in more vertical industrial sectors. Second, in view of the increasing popularity of cloud service models, it is indispensable to explore the collaboration theories and methods to implement service-oriented integration to promote the transformation and upgrading of the Smart Court SoSs engineering from self-built systems to shared services. Third, it is crucial to combine the direction of advanced technologies, such as artificial intelligence, 5G, blockchain, and meta-universe, to improve the adaptability and flexibility of the framework, and to enable deeper integration of advanced science and technologies to judicial operations. Finally, the construction and enrichment of the theoretical system dynamics of information systems can provide sufficient scientific support. Meanwhile, in addition to the technical implementation, the construction of Smart Court inevitably involves user feedback, reform of the judicial system, establishment of related systems and norms, etc. Enforcing the research work on the integration of science and technology, legal theory, and social sciences, will certainly provide more powerful support for the construction of Smart Court in China to achieve more promising results.

6.5 Chapter Summary

The Smart Court SoSs engineering project of China inherit the experiences and methodologies of traditional system engineering. Based on the original basic theories, such as the universal information model, information metric system, the key evaluation indicators of information system-of-systems are put forward. The Smart Court system-of-systems project has fully reshaped the operation mode of the People's Court. Through continuous monitoring and monthly analysis of a series of key evaluation indicators, the entire information system-of-systems is in a good state of progressive development and constant optimization, making an important contribution to the progress of judicial civilization in the information era. The exploration and practice of key evaluation indicators of information system-of-systems under fundamental information theories, and quality efficiency improvement are not only applicable to the vertical sectors of Smart Court but also provide useful references for e-government, as well as other large-scale information projects.

References

1. Xu, J., Sun, F., Chen, Q.: Introduction to Smart Court System Engineering (in Chinese). People's Court Press, Beijing (2021)
2. Jamshidi, M.: System of Systems Engineering: Innovations for the 21st Century. John Wiley & Sons, Hoboken (2009)
3. Xu, J., Liu, Z., Wang, S., et al.: Foundations and applications of information systems dynamics. Engineering. **4**, 18 (2002). https://doi.org/10.1016/j.eng.2022.04.018

Postscript

Information, matter and energy constitute the real world organically. In the world, matter is an objective reality that does not depend on human subjective consciousness. Energy is the ability of matter to move without relying on human subjective consciousness. Information uses matter or energy as a medium to reflect the objective world and the subjective world. The nature of things and the laws of their movement patterns show the way of existence and movement of matter, with objective materiality. From the the trinity of matter, energy, and information in the real world, the information reflects the nature of things in the world and the law of movement, to solve fundamental theoretical problems in information science, such as the essence of information, measurement methods, model algorithms, and controllability of calculations.

Objective information theory is based on the triadic theory of matter, energy, and information and the application requirements of information systems. We put forward the definition of the connotation, constituent elements, nature, characteristics and basic metrics of information, which are specifically exemplified through the Air Traffic Control System and the Smart Court. As the research is at a relatively shallow level, there is still a lot of theoretical exploration that needs to be deepened, such as the structural connection between the information constituent elements, especially the state set and the reflection set, and the mutual influence of the basic measures of information. Constraint relations, the corresponding relations between various information metrics and information system operation links, etc., need to be studied using more extensive mathematics and system science theories, to truly establish compliance with the laws of nature and the development trend of information technology, and be able to guide the development of information systems.

Now that information has penetrated our study, work and life, big data analysis and mining is a weapon to give full play to its value, and it is also difficult. Nonetheless, "it is already a cliff with hundreds of feet of ice, and there are still beautiful things." We must work hard to innovate and overcome difficulties. "Suddenly like a spring breeze, thousands of trees and pears bloom." We look forward to breakthrough results in this area of research.

J. Xu et al., *Objective Information Theory*, SpringerBriefs in Computer Science,
https://doi.org/10.1007/978-981-19-9929-1

Printed in the United States
by Baker & Taylor Publisher Services